Life Lessons From My Father

by

Eugene L. Moore,

Ph.D. Candidate

Life To Legacy, LLC

Life2Legacy.com

Life Lessons From My Father

Copyright © 2015 by Eugene L. Moore

ISBN-13 978-1-939654-46-5

ISBN-10 1939654467

All Scripture quotations, unless otherwise indicated are taken from the New International Version®, NIV® Copyright © 1973, 1978, 1984, 2011 by Biblica, Inc.® Used by permission. All rights reserved worldwide.
Scripture identified NKJV are taken from the New King James Version®. Copyright © 1982 by Thomas Nelson. Used by permission. All rights reserved.
Scripture identified ESV are taken from English Standard Version Copyright © 2001 by Crossway Bibles, a publishing ministry of Good News Publishers.
Scripture identified NASB taken from the New American Standard Bible Copyright © 1960, 1962, 1963, 1968, 1971, 1972, 1973, 1975, 1977, 1995 by The Lockman Foundation.
Scripture identified ISV are taken from the International Standard Version Copyright © 1995-2014 by ISV Foundation. All Rights Reserved Internationally. Used by permission of Davidson Press, LLC.
Scripture identified LB are taken form the Living Bible copyright © 1971 by Tyndale House Foundation. Used by permission of Tyndale House Publishers Inc., Carol Stream, Illinois 60188. All rights reserved.
Scripture identified NLT are taken from New Living Translation copyright© 1996, 2004, 2007, 2013 by Tyndale House Foundation. Used by permission of Tyndale House Publishers Inc., Carol Stream, Illinois 60188. All rights reserved.
Scripture identified MSG are taken from The Message. Copyright © 1993, 1994, 1995, 1996, 2000, 2001, 2002. Used by permission of NavPress Publishing Group.

Printed in the United States
10 9 8 7 6 5 4 3 2 1

Front cover design by: Treviante Brown

Published by: Life To Legacy, LLC
2441 Vermont Street, #57
Blue Island, IL 60406
877-267-7477
Life2legacybooks@att.net

CONTENTS

Presented To

Send Emails to:
info@assurancecreekyouth.org

About the Author

Eugene L. Moore is a current doctoral student in Education Policy, Organization and Leadership at the University of Illinois at Urbana-Champaign, where he has received both his master's and bachelor's in Human Resources and Communication respectively. Born and raised in Chicago, Illinois in a single parent home, he has witnessed firsthand the consequences of not having a quality education. Fortunately, he received a scholarship from the Daniel Murphy Scholarship Foundation to attend the prestigious Providence St. Mel School (PSM) located on Chicago's West Side, which for nearly forty years had 100% of its graduates accepted to four-year colleges and universities.

Upon graduating from PSM, he received a four-year scholarship to the University of Illinois from College Bound, which is currently in operation as Chicago Scholars. This program is aimed at providing needed resources to underserved high school students by giving them access to a quality educational experience.

Eugene attributes his success to his relationship with God, the influence of his mother, grandmother, mentors, teachers, and his inner determination to think beyond his circumstances. He prides himself on giving back and has contributed to various organizations and institutions committed to service, education, and health both domestically and globally. He established an annual scholarship at the University of Illinois, which bears the names of his mother and grandmother. However, his biggest contribution to service is the founding of the nonprofit Assurance Creek Youth Program (ACYP) in 2012, where he serves as the President and Chief Executive Officer. ACYP is birthed out of his experiences with great mentors and excellent educational institutions. It is his hope that Assurance Creek Youth Program will become an organization that inspires youth to unlock the greatness that lives inside of them and reach their God-given potential.

Humble by nature, Eugene L. Moore is not interested in creating a spotlight that only highlights his accomplishments, but believes his greatest legacy will come from the success of those whom he has aimed to inspire.

ACKNOWLEDGEMENTS

My heavenly Father has orchestrated a life for me filled with boundless opportunities. For that, I say thank you.

My family serves as my inspiration to strengthen future generations. For that, I say thank you.

My mother, Diane Moore, has been an integral part in my success, from making sure my belt was neatly fastened to demanding that I spoke with great articulation and conviction. For that, I say thank you.

My mentors have served as great examples of success. Paul J. Adams III, Gary Caplan, Marc Grayson, Todd Grayson, Joel Massel, Samuel Mendenhall, Jim Murphy, John Russell, and Emmett Vaughn have provided their time, advice, and resources. For that, I say thank you.

My teachers provided a space for me to explore my intellectual inquisitiveness. Amanda Keroes and Sharon Mixon were beyond exceptional and exemplified the power of great teachers. For that, I say thank you.

Alfred Kentigern Siewers, Associate Professor at Bucknell University, encouraged me as an undergraduate student to pursue writing. For that, I say thank you.

James D. Anderson Gutgsell, Professor at University of Illinois, and Laurence Parker, Professor at University of Utah, were supporters of my desire to pursue my doctorate. For that, I say thank you.

Dr. Dennis Woods and Life to Legacy Books moved this project forward with diligence and compassion. For that, I say thank you.

Finally, there will always be people who you fail to acknowledge, but just because your name is not mentioned, that does not mean you are not appreciated for your understanding and encouragement. For that, I say thank you.

FOREWORD I

It is hard today to look at all the chaos and tragedies, the broken relationships, families, and lives. It's tough to stand for Christ as evil seems to triumph over humanity, and you try to explain how God if He is who He says He is, could allow these things to happen. The question comes to mind, "Why doesn't He do something about it if He's God?"

If this is not your question, it certainly is the question of multitudes. Is there an answer to the pain, the disappointment, the headache you and countless others are facing? Yes, my friend, there is an answer. God is big enough to handle your questions and strong enough to deliver you from pain and doubt. You will find your guide to life's challenges and triumphs in this book because it will introduce you to the Book of books. It isn't coincidence that you have this book in your hands and are reading the words on this page. All of your life's events were orchestrated for you to be right here at this very moment.

I have read many daily inspirational books, and most have a sameness to them. They tell you things you already know and sometimes make you feel bad for not having already done those things you knew to do. This book doesn't make you feel that way. I know a lot about what God's purpose is for my life, but I learned a lot from this book.

I've known Eugene Moore for a few years now, and he's always had a way with words. I work as an Academic Advisor in the College of Education at the University of Illinois. I am also in the final stages of my doctoral program in, Education Policy, Organization and Leadership. Eugene is a striking guy with a commanding presence, always immaculately dressed. Underneath the outward appearance, he is a regular guy who has had more than his share of struggles. As a result of those struggles, he has an unusual commitment to the gospel and to encouraging this generation of young people.

Such commitment can be found in his program, Assurance Creek Youth Program (ACYP), in which he is the President. Unlike so many youth leaders of our time, he doesn't take a populist approach that looks to blame others for the bad things that happen to our young people. Eugene believes you can be the answer to your own situation if you have knowledge and discipline.

Eugene oftentimes visits my office and is a particularly calming voice of reason during the most stressful, panicked, and taxing days. Have you ever met a person that you know would provide a word of comfort no matter the situation? Eugene is that individual, and I'm grateful that he has chosen to put his words of wisdom in a book to comfort the hearts of people around the globe. If you put into practice the life lessons from this book, it will make the things regular folks lose sleep over seem manageable. I could see myself and relate to each of Eugene's topics in this book.

Even though, I might not have had that exact experience. And in case you didn't have that experience, Eugene does a great job of giving you spiritual tips, if life happens to place you there. Eugene's goal in this book is not just to help you learn the life lessons from the Father, but to one day be able to teach others the lessons of the Father. For Eugene, the loop isn't complete if you don't give back.

You have searched for a book like this for a long time. A book that empowers you even if you don't have inspirational literature, daily meditation, a prayer life, a father, or any kind of spiritual guidance in your life right now. I encourage you to read this book, fix your situation, and learn the lesson.

Joe Cross, Ph.D. Candidate
Academic Advisor
University of Illinois

Now to him who is able to do far more abundantly than all that we ask or think, according to the power at work within us...   *Ephesians 3:20ESV*

FOREWORD II

The first day I was formally introduced to Mr. Eugene L. Moore, I knew he loved God, as his actions displayed such compassion for the well-being of others. I soon learned he had left the corporate sector to pursue his doctorate. But what was even more compelling was his commitment to service. I discovered his research, teaching, and service were intricately linked to form a platform of solidarity positioned to provide opportunities for the underrepresented. He always seems to find a way to remind those he encounters of the power of having faith in the promises of God. He firmly believes everyone has a unique gift and purpose in life.

Eugene chooses to share his gift through his motivational writings in hopes of encouraging others to succeed. He aims to explore and connect complicated historical events, biblical references, knowledge and lived experiences as a way to emphasize the importance of believing and allowing a higher power to navigate your path. In his latest book Life Lessons from My Father, he places his wisdom in a collection of short narratives that provide deep insight into some of life's most challenging situations by providing practical solutions. It serves as an important portal to remembering our humanity and need for service. The thoughts and quotes linked together in this remarkable collage of narratives are providing a way for its readers to remain connected to the joy of living and reaching their divine potential. Readers will find themselves on an emotional journey, giving them a newfound motivation to conquer fear and focus on self-reflection.

Desiree Y. McMillion, Ph.D. Candidate

PREFACE

Life Lessons from My Father aims to add a more robust level of encouragement for readers who are searching for inspiration that goes beyond just making them feel better about their situation and compels them to take action. The book heavily relies on biblical principles and attempts to dispel any myths about the Christian walk being easy. Furthermore, it hopes to reach all different types of people, ranging from those who aspire to be successful to those who are greatly accomplished.

There are countless books about self-help, inspiration, and encouragement and this book undoubtedly falls within those categories. But in these pages, readers are given the tools needed to not only secure success but also to sustain it for years to come. The book is a collection of short narratives that cover many of life's issues. It had no specific theme but was created organically from messages made apparent by God. It is my hope that these reflections bring some level of inspiration and insight for whatever life presents.

Blessed is the one who perseveres under trial because, having stood the test, that person will receive the crown of life that the Lord has promised to those who love him. James 1:12

REFLECTION 1

A MAN WITHOUT HIS EXAMPLE

A boy who grows up without a father has to look outside of his mother's nurturing ability, as he instinctively knows that despite her sincere efforts to provide safety, she will never truly fill the role of his father. A father's absence can be due to various circumstances: divorce, separation, the father being unaware he has fathered a child, death, or the father simply refusing to care for his child. Unfortunately, many mothers have to contend with this unnatural reality. A child can only be born of a man and a woman, and a father's absence is always felt; no matter how great a mother a child is afforded. I am not suggesting a child cannot receive love from various sources, nor am I trying to diminish the role that single mothers play to influence, encourage, and support their children in the absence of their father. I am suggesting that we are mindful of the intimate relationships we form prior to birthing children into the world.

Fortunately, manhood can be learned through positive role models coupled with a great relationship with your heavenly Father. A strong mother will always recruit positive male role models into her child's life, as she knows her perspective is different from that of a man. A single father has the same challenges, as he unequivocally understands he can never be his child's mother. Therefore, for all those children without fathers in the home, you can connect with positive role models and develop a strong relationship with God. By doing so, you can miraculously fill the void left by your absent father. When you are well into adulthood, I am sure some will ask how you became such a strong man, and you can humbly respond that despite my father's absence, I became a man without his example.

INTERROGATE YOUR ENTOURAGE

It is important for celebrities, as well as those without fame, to understand that when attempting to create a magnanimous image, it will inherently invite an entourage. Thus, most high profile celebrities travel with an entourage. Celebrities are bombarded with a heavy influx of media attention, which perhaps necessitates their need for an entourage as a form of protection for their physical safety and image. However, success does not have to travel with an entourage to display its merit, but uses results as its greatest validation. You can spend your entire life surrounding yourself with lots of people, only to discover most of them are around for personal gain. Therefore, it is imperative that you interrogate your entourage to figure out who are true assets and which ones are liabilities. Many celebrities learn a valuable lesson in that people will stand with you in your success or fame but are absent in your failure.

Circle of Friends

Our environment plays a critical role in our well-being. As we journey throughout life, we quickly discover we cannot change people but we do have the power to change the people we choose to have in our circle. Your circle must be equipped with individuals who appreciate the truth, believe in a greater power, are confident in their own abilities, and operate from a reciprocal stance, knowing their role was never intended to be only that of a recipient of love, but of a giver as well. Your circle of friends will either hinder or elevate your potential, and we must all choose wisely.

Never Too Late

A child needs and deserves a father. We have seen the positive images of a father walking his daughter down the aisle, a father screaming as his son makes a game-winning play, or a father watching his child receive their college degree. Unfortunately, the absent father is not associated with such positive images. He is represented by the tears that flow down his daughter's face as her uncle walks her down the aisle; or by the longing of a boy who, although his coach is great, wishes his father cared as much for him; or by the sadness of a child when cheers of loved ones at big moments like graduation can be silenced by a father's absence. For those fathers who have accepted their role with pride, we commend you. For those who have shunned their responsibility, we say it is never too late to be a father.

Eugene L. Moore

Perception is Reality

Your perception of the world is intrinsically based on your environment. For example, young children in a poorly resourced community are less likely to see successful people within their community. Unfortunately, interacting with teachers, physicians, clerks, or other professionals within the community does not negate the negative realities which invade these communities, like a high concentration of crime, poverty, and inadequate schools. Those professionals who serve the community are likely to live outside the neighborhoods in which they are employed. As the bell rings and the time clock is punched, they escape to their environments of comfort that, are often void of these deplorable distractions.

Therefore, when a young child states their dream is to become a taxi-cab driver, let us not focus on the lack of depth of their dreams but on the inherent limitations of their environment. We believe excuses have no rightful place within the realms of success but we must not solely focus on those few individuals who rose above these circumstances. Although, education plays a pivotal factor in eradicating social ills, we must not be so naïve as to believe that education alone can solve the many systemic issues which plague these communities

God is with You

In life, we have limited control over the things that affect us. For example, we cannot control the opinions of others or unforeseen tragedy. In reality, our greatest sense of agency comes from how we react to a particular situation. When tragedy ensues, is it our default reaction to blame others and become frustrated or do we look for possible strategies and solutions to confront the circumstance? We must learn that even in the greatest moments of despair we still have victory. If we decide to offer what we have to those in need, no matter how meager, we provide God with the room needed to miraculously bring it to a level of abundance.

Maybe you have lost someone or something of great value and the hope for tomorrow seems so bleak. But staying on this emotional roller-coaster is not a great demonstration of your faith. Breathe, cry, scream, but through it all, trust that God will deliver. It hurts and it should. When you look back on it all, you will quickly discern that, even though, the pain seemed insurmountable, you survived. Use this moment as the start of something new, and not only will His angels travel with you throughout the race, but God will meet you at the finish line. There is a triumph in every tragedy. Be blessed and know that God is with you always.

The Journey of Life

Life is truly a journey, and it varies for each individual. But if you desire peace, you must not be consumed by the frailties of life. In reality, we can find ourselves in places where we are uncomfortable, lose people whom we love, and watch our youthfulness slip away. When you decide to embrace the precious moments of life, you will never be stuck in the past. Your youth can turn into wisdom. Your attractiveness can turn into esteemed elegance. Losing a special person can become a memoir of love. Life does have inherent frailties, but it is always about your perspective. Live life to the fullest and future generations will benefit because you lived with purpose. This is your truth. This is your peace. This is your legacy. This is the journey of life.

WE THE PEOPLE

Moral consciousness is the ability to discern right from wrong. Throughout our lives, we will face many decisions that require us to respond in such a way that others will quickly learn our commitment to character, integrity, justice, and truth. Our nation is often polarized around many issues like religion, race, political affiliation, sexual orientation, gender, power, and much more. This polarization can become the fuel for inequality and showcases our moral consciousness as a nation. Our responsibility as humans should always be to help those in need and not allow anyone to suffer unnecessary pain. Maybe one day our rhetoric will change, and we will truly be a nation of inclusion, not only through legal prowess and ideology but also within the hearts of all citizens. We the people must fervently believe that all people are created equal. To this, we say, God Bless you and God Bless the United States of America.

FACING THE DAY

What if today is the day that your life takes an unexpected turn for the worse? Do you instantly blame others and feel defeated? The reality is we have little or no control over what happens to us, but our greatest sense of agency is how we respond to the situation. Misfortune seems to rob us of our happiness, but it most certainly does not have to decrease our faith, truth, resolve, or peace. The moment we decide to have peace with whatever the situation creates, we allow God to bring joy to our most precarious realities. While our ultimate prayer is that negativity eludes us, the Bible states, "Man who is born of a woman is of few days and full of trouble" (Job 14:1 ESV). But God ultimately turns trouble into triumph. And the Bible says, "Blessed is the one who perseveres under trial because, having stood the test, that person will receive the crown of life that the Lord has promised to those who love him" (James 1:12).

SELF-REFLECTION

Generally, selfishness is not considered to be an admirable trait. But there are times in which focusing on one's self is the best option for internal happiness and success. To give to others is rewarding and in fact, pleases God, but it does not negate the importance of being well and loving yourself. We all lack perfection. If we link giving to perfection, then our giving will be limited and pretentious. Therefore, we must make an effort to become our personal best. In order to achieve this goal, we must endure self-reflection. Some might consider this selfish, but if you desire to give more, you must first become well. If going inward causes you to become a better friend, spouse, parent, sibling, coworker, Christian, and simply a better person, then I implore you to take a moment and be selfish because we all benefit when you are well.

Jesus looked at them and said, "With man this is impossible, but with God all things are possible."

Matthew 19:26

REFLECTION 2

EMBRACE THE NOW

Yesterday, while it might have been amazing or disastrous, cannot be altered but only serves as a past event. Tomorrow is solely based on speculation for we have no clue what the day will entail, but we must be prayerful it will greet us with joy. Therefore, the only time we have is now. But many of us are so consumed with the past and the future that we shamefully miss the present. Allow today to be the day you seize the moment, embrace your talents, acknowledge your weaknesses, and persevere despite what the day offers. God gave us this moment. Regardless of our circumstances, we must be thankful that we have been given another day to become better. Live each day with love and humility, for life is simply a gift.

SILENCE YOUR CRITICS

When you decide to reach your potential, you must also be willing to endure many obstacles. It is ironic that those who possess the greatest talents often have the greatest critics. Those who have made a conscious decision to succeed understand that they will hear "no" countless times and are likely to fail before success materializes but their resilience is their greatest attribute.

On March 28, 1995, Michael Jordan entered New York's Madison Square Garden, playing his fifth game since his return to basketball. Although he typically played well in New York, his previous games had been disappointing, and sports writers speculated his talents had diminished. As history tells us, Jordan scored fifty-five points, and he was the cover story of nearly every newspaper in the country, with the caption "Double Nickel." That is what success looks like. Successful people boldly confront their critics, not with convoluted rhetoric but with factual evidence that silences those who doubted their ability to succeed. Your potential is your greatest strength and your critics' greatest fear. Today is the game of your life and you must play to win. What will be your highlights?

THE DREAM DEFINED

On August 28, 1963, Dr. Martin Luther King Jr. addressed the nation with Abraham Lincoln serving as the backdrop for his famed "I have A Dream" speech. It is now more than half a century later since his iconic speech. King's legacy is deeper than this speech. But we must use his words, which state, "injustice anywhere is a threat to justice everywhere." We have made tremendous progress, but there is definitely more work needed. Women must be paid equally, voter suppression cannot be tolerated, education needs to be equitable, poverty needs to be eliminated, and discrimination in all forms must be eradicated.

King only lived to be thirty-nine. John F. Kennedy lived to be forty-six. Jesus lived to be thirty-three. As we know, life is short. But having longevity does not guarantee that you make your mark on the world.

In fact, we can accomplish more if we live our lives with the intensity of knowing the time for change happens in the present moment. To all youngsters around the world, we ask what is your dream and what will be your legacy? Today is the day you make history. Dream bigger than your circumstances and rely on God to allow those dreams to materialize. I have a dream that we will all believe we are greater than our circumstances.

CONFIDENT SUCCESS

Confidence does not boast, brag, or belittle but instead is strategic, bold, and resilient. People often confuse confidence with arrogance, but there is certainly a distinction between the terms. An arrogant person relies solely on their perceived power, ability to intimidate, and the weaknesses of others. A confident person is humble, but they are fully cognizant of their abilities. They pay little to no attention to others, as they unequivocally understand that the opinion of others has no credence.

Lastly, it is important to be aware of three other types of people: fakers, takers, and haters. Fakers are not authentic but are simply imposters. Takers are those who recognize your talents as an opportunity for their benefit. Haters are often friends or people who are close to you, but they only hope for your failure. As a confident person, you are mindful of these types of people but you welcome them because if you do not have fakers, takers, and haters, it is likely that you are not reaching your greatest potential. Success has many rewards but is inherently consequential.

Seize it

Opportunity sometimes just presents itself, but more often, those who desire it seize it. If your life seemingly lacks opportunities, ask yourself whether you have been passive or fearful. A passive person wants better but is reluctant to speak on their behalf, which gives them little opportunities. A fearful person lives in continual doubt and believes they are not good enough. If you desire more for yourself, you must make a conscious decision to do more. Being passive and fearful can lead to bitterness and blame. Decide today to seize and create opportunities for yourself. In reality, you cannot make a shot you never attempted to take. Success is contingent on trying. Never stop trying or believing in yourself. Unleash opportunities and boldly face your fears.

See Beyond Your Circumstances

Sometimes our experiences, whether good, bad or indifferent, can limit our understanding of God's power. God's options are simply greater than any of our experiences, and to limit Him to our unique circumstances is not wise. Many years ago, a young boy had a mass the size of a grapefruit on his brain. His health was so severe that nurses manually gave him oxygen through an attached breathing apparatus. The doctors placed an x-ray of the mass on the screen and were simply astonished by the image. Doctors informed the parents that they had no expertise with a case of this magnitude and suggested the young boy be transported by helicopter to another hospital. The parents, along with the entire church, community, family, and friends began to pray. Within hours, doctors retook the x-ray of the young boy's brain, only to discover that the mass had totally dissipated. The young boy's health quickly recovered and he was released days later and returned to his fifth-grade classroom.

Man's options are limited and displeasing, but God's options are always limitless and beyond our expectations. Therefore, where ever your circumstances or your experiences have brought you, it is simply no indication of where God can take you. Jesus says, "With man this is impossible but with God all things are possible" (Matthew 19:26).

BE ACCOUNTABLE

Accountability is a struggle for some people, as it inherently implies that you bear some of the responsibility for your circumstances. It is easier to blame a parent who abandoned you, a teacher who discouraged you, a friend who betrayed you, a system that diminishes you, a God who you believe does not hear you, and a partner or spouse who has hurt you. The reality is that in every situation within your life, the only one consistent person is yourself. The moment you begin to focus on the one person you can change is when your life will begin to take a different direction. To blame others for your failed relationships, poor decisions, negative attitude, lack of motivation, or just your overall circumstances is an excuse.

The Bible says, "So then, each of us will give an account of himself to God" (Romans 14:12). Today release the blame and begin to rebuild your life for the enemy desires to destroy your destiny. When you fail to be accountable, your progress is impeded, and the enemy is allowed to distract you. We all fall short; it is what makes us human but if we would only humble ourselves. And the Bible says, "When pride comes, then comes disgrace, but with humility comes wisdom" (Proverbs 11:2). Be wise and be accountable.

Unwavering Trust

> Trust in the Lord with all your heart and lean not on your own understanding; in all your ways submit to him, and he will make your paths straight.
>
> Proverbs 3:5-6

It is often said that men are unlikely to ask for directions, even when they know they are lost. Being in a car with someone who refuses to seek help at the expense of your time is unproductive. Men are not the only culprits of failing to seek counsel. We all as Christians sometimes forget we serve a God, who has the ability to make our crooked paths straight. We trust and have faith in many things, like faith that our new car will start, that the wall on which we are leaning will not collapse, or that our check will be rendered after we have submitted our time to payroll. The reality is that placing your trust in man is always a losing bet. How many times have you left your raincoat because of what the weatherman said, only to find yourself in a storm later? Or maybe you were told in error that you had the job or promotion, or that the cancer was in remission. Unlike man, God cannot tell a lie or fail, for He is always victorious.

Today, despite the situation or what man has said, trust in the Lord and He will place you on the path to greatness. To silence the enemy we must have unwavering faith and trust God to provide. Your breakthrough is here now. Stand and watch God instantaneously move you to the front of the line. Get Ready!

RSVP YOUR ENEMY

You prepare a table before me in the presence of my enemies. You anoint my head with oil; my cup overflows.   Psalm 23:5

"Sit at my right hand until I make your enemies a footstool for your feet."   Psalm 110:1

No weapon formed against you shall prosper. Isaiah 54:17 NKJV

These three scriptures are pivotal to your success and well-being. While they are all heavily referenced, it is important that we understand them in their totality. We live in a time where people have coined the word "hater," which means someone who despises your success, accomplishments, or just the nature of your being. The word hater is a mere replacement for the word enemy.

Seeing that these two words are synonymous, you can use the term hater in the first two scriptures, and the meaning would be the same. Therefore, God invites your haters to your celebration, but their role is not one of comfort—they will serve as a footstool for your feet. God places them in a position of submission and servitude solely because they hated you for loving Him. Never be dismayed by those who hate you but love them until God places them in their rightful position, which is at your feet. Success comes with a lot of responsibilities and it also comes with jealousy, sacrifice, and pain. However, if you remain rooted in God, He will use the negative for your positive outcome.

Finally, the third scripture lets us know that the "hater's" primary job is to form weapons. But what good is a weapon that only malfunctions?

Today, embrace your enemy and get ready for your party. Your cup is overflowing, which means that God has a blessing so big you cannot even contain it. Are you distracted, are you worried, or are you ready? If you are in fact ready, please know that God already has a RSVP list of your enemies. It is time to celebrate!

IT'S PRUNING SEASON

> I am the true vine, and my Father is the gardener. He cuts off every branch in me that bears no fruit, while every branch that does bear fruit he prunes so that it will be even more fruitful.   John 15:1-2

As a child, when you come home from your first day of school and your parents ask you to name your friends, the list is exhaustive. Everyone is your friend. As you continue to grow, the list, which was once abundant is now extremely small, and for some it's non-existent. A true friend is rare and a gift from God. If you have been fortunate enough to have a true friend, then your focus should always be on appreciating their friendship and not taking advantage of their love. However, many people desire to have lots of friends, but at a cost greater than they can reasonably afford.

A gardener prunes for several reasons: the branch may have died, the plant might be weakened or diseased, and in some cases, the growth is premature and must be pruned to maximize growth. How can we apply this biblical scripture to our daily lives? In an effort to make this relative to your unique situation, imagine your best friend in elementary school, high school, college, or work. In most cases, those who were with us in our early years of life have departed from our inner circle. These departures are often due to the growth of one of the individuals and the inability of the other to move forward. Just like the gardener prunes, so does God. Your success is contingent on God's pruning ability and your willingness to welcome the cut. If you knew that your breakthrough was being blocked because you were unwilling to cut an unproductive, negative, emotionally unbalanced or even a good friend, would you welcome the pruning?

Today, look back over your life and see how God has placed you through the pruning process. Think about your immediate reaction to the pruning process and ask yourself were you upset, bitter, or grateful. God is about to take you to a place that is so great and filled with abundance, but He must prune away those dead, weak, and unproductive things. It is time for you to reach your destiny. The reality is that some of your so-called friends are not meant to be with you at the next level. Think of an elevator. It has a capacity limit. If you exceed the requirement, you jeopardize your safety and cannot make it to your destination. It is okay to be a team of one as long as you have the Father, Son, and Holy Spirit. If you want to grow, sometimes others have to go!

Therefore do not worry about tomorrow, for tomorrow will worry about itself. Each day has enough trouble of its own.   *Matthew 6:34*

Reflection 3

No Need To Worry

Therefore I tell you, do not worry about your life, what you will eat or drink; or about your body, what you will wear. Is not life more than food and the body more than clothes? Look at the birds of the air; they do not sow or reap or store away in barns, and yet your heavenly Father feeds them. Are you just as valuable as they? Can any one of you by worrying add a single hour to your life? Therefore do not worry about tomorrow, for tomorrow will worry about itself. Each day has enough trouble of its own. Matthew 6:25-27, 34

Most children live with little concern about the frailties of life. When you are five years old, a mortgage, stress from the job, failed relationships, insecurities, financial burdens, getting accepted into a particular program, residual pain, and many other daunting issues never enter your purview. Therefore, one of the great things about being a child is that you have no concept or understanding of what it means to worry. In a real sense, worrying is a learned behavior that intensifies when you fail to trust in the Lord.

As you enter adolescence (or even earlier for some), you become more familiar with worrying. The world gifts us with images of beauty, success, prestige, and all the things society deems as worthy. But as Christ's followers, we are not of this world. When we attempt to follow the mandates of the world, we often worry if we are good enough if we will be accepted, and if we will be happy if we acquire more things. The answers to these questions are a resounding no. If money, success, prestige, or fame where the pinnacle of happiness, then we could look to Hollywood for answers. But we know Hollywood has its issues, like suicide, mental illness, addiction, adultery, depression, and much more. Therefore, we must rely on the Lord to strengthen us and not allow ourselves to go down the slippery slope of worrying. Birds soar in the air. Wild animals graze the land. Insects crawl about the ground and fly through the wind. Yet worrying is not their function. They solely rely on God to provide. Are we not greater than the pigeon, the squirrel, or the crafty ant?

The scripture is clear and the message is unwavering because God chastises our logic and implores us to elevate our thinking. Whether today represents trouble or triumph, your worrying does not enhance the day. The enemy loves when we worry because it takes us away from God. Trust in Him, for He is preparing a feast in your honor. Do not be distracted or dismayed by your circumstances but watch God birth your next breakthrough. How hungry are you for God to provide a miracle? You are next in line! Learn to make worry wait and focus on Him. He can, He will, He has, and in Jesus' name, it is done. Amen!

SHINE YOUR LIGHT

"You are the light of the world. A town built on a hill cannot be hidden. Neither do people light a lamp and put it under a bowl. Instead they put it on its stand, and it gives light to everyone in the house. In the same way, let your light shine before men, that they may see your good deeds and glorify your Father in heaven."

Matthew 5:14-16

Composer and teacher Harry Dixon Loes wrote what is now an iconic gospel song titled, "This Little Light of Mine," which has been featured in numerous films and sampled by several recording artists. Both the song and scripture seem to represent some level of arrogance, but such an assertion is far from the truth. In fact, shining your light is a sign of humility, for it represents your reverence to God. The world boasts about its accomplishments and record-breaking feats. As Christians, should we be silent about how God has shown favor in our lives? Such an assumption is ill-fated and unproductive. If God blessed you with good health, family, friends, a promotion, a unique talent or skill, a home, prosperity, an education, happiness and joy, peace, or even riches, then to be silent is to tell God you are ashamed of what He has done. Actually, we try to make others feel comfortable at the expense of displeasing God.

If you have a true friend who has recently lost a job but you have received a promotion, then they will be happy for you because they see how God has blessed you. If you have a true friend who is struggling with their weight and you are able to eat as you please without gaining a pound, then they will be happy that you do not have the same struggle. If you have a true friend who has not completed college but you are highly educated, they will thank God for your success and accept their life decisions without resenting you in the process. If you are around people with whom you are hesitant to share your dreams and accomplishments, then perhaps you need to change the people around you.

Today let your light shine, no matter how small or great. The light in a refrigerator is small in wattage but sufficient for the space that it illuminates. A baseball field has massive lights that illuminate in the darkness of night and fill the vastness of the space. The reality is that the faintest light shines in complete darkness. The more you let your light shine, the more light God will place inside of you. Open your mouth, profess with intensity the goodness of God, and watch Him light your path toward greatness. Silence your enemies by blinding them with your light!

MISGUIDED LOYALTY

A friend loves at all times, and a brother is born for a time of adversity.   Proverbs 17:17

A man of many companions may come to ruin, but there is a friend who sticks closer than a brother.   Proverbs 18:24 ESV

Actor and recording artist Tyrese Gibson stated, "Loyalty has an expiration date." Where are your loyalties positioned? Oftentimes we place a great deal of trust and loyalty in our family and so-called friends but after continual abuse and a lack of appreciation, we soon discover we must remove ourselves from the table of our enemies. Once you remove yourself from the table of your enemies, you might have some regrets and perhaps even some guilt. But ask yourself one pertinent question: who was feeding you? It can be difficult to walk away from a parent, a friend, or a family member, but if you continue to invite drama in your life, you will continuously live in chaos. Your enemies are consistent in their plot against you, which is to kill, steal, and destroy your destiny.

Tyrese was speaking about his mother, who had been an alcoholic for as long as he could remember, and how he stopped talking to her for nearly a year to cleanse himself of their toxic relationship. In a real sense, those closest to us could be in fact the most threatening to us if we are not careful and willing to make immediate changes. Jesus was willing to make immediate changes, saying to his beloved disciple Peter, "Get behind me, Satan! You are a stumbling block to me; you do not have in mind the things of God, but merely human concerns" (Matthew 16:23). We have heard the story of Judas, the one who betrayed Jesus, which seems to be the most egregious act among his disciples but Jesus never called him Satan. He called Peter, who many would consider the most loyal apostle, Satan. Hence, if my being loyal to you causes me to stumble, then you are not my friend but my enemy. Jesus greeted Judas with a kiss, for He understood that if your betrayal leads to my resurrection, then I welcome your schemes. But for Peter, Jesus' mindset was when your actions impede my destiny, then I know you are my enemy.

Today, whom will you kiss and whom will you rebuke? Do not confuse

God allowing a necessary evil with a true enemy! Jesus is the friend we need in our lives, for He will be closer to us than a brother and He will never forsake us but will always be with us in the darkness of the valley and during the sunshine of the mountain top.

We are wise not to consume spoiled milk or outdated poultry, but when will we be wise enough to realize that loyalty too has an expiration date? It is time to remove the outdated and spoiled items from the pantries and refrigerators of our souls. How long will you feed your enemies? Get up from the table and walk into your destiny, where your enemies serve you and do not eat!

HAPPINESS IN GOD

Instruct those who are rich in this present world not to be conceited or to fix their hope on the uncertainty of riches, but on God, who richly supplies us with all things to enjoy.

1 Timothy 6:17 NASB

You will make known to me the path of life; In Your presence is fullness of joy; In Your right hand there are pleasures forever.

Psalm 16:11 NASB

A common misconception is that being rich will bring you an instant level of happiness. But those who have wealth understand that money has limits. Within the memoirs of many famous people, they write of how their riches could not rid them of their loneliness. Imagine living in a sprawling mansion with servants, luxury automobiles, rare paintings adorning the walls, and a master suite the size of a modest

New York home, but internally you feel alone. It would not be a fair assertion that all rich people are void of happiness nor would it be appropriate to suggest that those without the riches of the world are prisoners of their financial woes. However, the scripture contends that riches are inherently uncertain and equating your happiness to your financial portfolio is unwise.

The richest person on the Forbes lists will ultimately depart from this world and leave their fortune to their heirs or beneficiaries. In a real sense, wealth can be transferred, but happiness is intrinsically linked to an individual and cannot be bartered, sold, or bequeathed to another person. Therefore, if money cannot buy happiness, where do we acquire its goodness? There is truly only one pathway to happiness, and it is through the grace of God.

How is it that you can visit a homeless shelter or an underdeveloped region in the world and find the greatest laughter, but in the gated community where wealth is abundant you can find misery? You often hear people speak negatively about the rich, but this level of rhetoric is unproductive and oftentimes comes from a place of envy and hatred. The Bible is clear that a rich person cannot buy season tickets to heaven, nor can a poor person pity their way into the kingdom.

Today we must decide to seek happiness. But be careful not to be fooled by the temporal nature of happiness. Truly, happiness is based on what is happening. For example, if money, relationships, health, family, friends, or even vanity fuels your happiness, what happens if all of a sudden your world changes? We must learn to seek God, as He is the only one who places happiness in our soul. Then despite the transitions of life, we can rest assured that He has pleasures for us which last forever. God is not a respecter of persons. He does not love a rich person more than He loves the lowly and downtrodden. Our God is awesome and delivers peace in the midst of your storm. If you desire true happiness, which will never fade, then decide today to accept Him even when times are difficult.

Perhaps your issue is not that you are not rich, but that you have not found true contentment in the Lord. He will richly supply all your needs! Be glad in Him and He will provide you with the breakthrough for which you have been praying. But He needs to know you love Him more than your desires. Do you want them more than you want Him? What happens if He does not grant your requests? Anyone can praise God when He says yes, but are you as enthused to praise Him when He says no? Happiness in God means you love Him even when you are carrying your cross of affliction.

Forgiveness is Freedom

And forgive us our debts, as we also have forgiven our debtors. And lead us not into temptation, but deliver us from the evil one. For if you forgive other people when they sin against you, your heavenly Father will also forgive you. But if you do not forgive others their sins, your Father will not forgive your sins.

Matthew 6:12-15

Bear with each other and forgive one another if any of you has a grievance against someone. Forgive as the Lord forgave you.

Colossians 3:13

As a child maybe you felt isolated and alone, abandoned by a parent, or even assaulted by someone you trusted. The late Lewis Smedes was a professor at Fuller Theological Seminary and had this to say about forgiveness, "To forgive is to set a prisoner free and discover the prisoner was you." Unfortunately, many people carry deep-seated resentment towards those who caused them pain. This behavior is unproductive and impedes one's ability to live life without bitterness, blame, and brokenness.

The questions of "Why me?" seem to infiltrate and impede your cognitive abilities, allowing you to be in a continually victimized state. Look in the mirror and face your pain because if you do not, you will become a prisoner without hope for freedom. Name those who have wronged you and boldly forgive them because you are better than the marred image of their destructive actions. "You intended to harm me, but God intended it for good to accomplish what is now being done, the saving of many lives" (Genesis 50:20). Daddy why did you leave us? Uncle Charles why did you touch me? Mom why did you not talk to me? Ms. Crawford why did you tell me I would never accomplish anything? You have been my friend for years, why did you betray me? Why did we divorce? Why? Why? Why?

The question of why can be exhaustive but the Bible tells us that the intention of harm does not mean God cannot use our pain as a testimony to uplift and encourage others. Finally, you can tell those who caused you pain these following statements, "I forgive you." You are not worth my freedom! You are not the only chapter of my life's narrative! You will no longer disrupt my emotions! I forgive you, for God forgave me. I pray He has mercy on your soul, for what you did to me was pure evil but through the miraculous grace of God I am good! I am no longer a prisoner of your pain!

GOD'S DEFINITION OF LOVE

Love is patient and kind; love does not envy or boast; it is not arrogant or rude. It does not insist on its own way; it is not irritable or resentful; it does not rejoice at wrongdoing, but rejoices with the truth. Love bears all things, believes all things, hopes all things, endures all things. 1 Corinthians 13:4-7 ESV

And now these three remain: faith, hope and love. But the greatest of these is love. 1 Corinthians 13:13

We hear the word love tossed around in our daily conversations with our spouse, partner, friends, family members, and others. But its use is often misrepresented. The Bible provides a clear definition of love, which we all should interrogate to decipher if those who claim to love us as God intends are sincere. Love is patient and kind, not impatient and unkind. Love does not envy or boast but is happy for those whom it confronts and has no desire to brag. Love is not arrogant or rude but operates with a sense of humility and respect. Love does not insist on its own way but is an ambassador for compromise. Love is not irritable or resentful but easygoing and accepting. Love does not rejoice at wrongdoing but is self-reflective and accountable, as it intends no harm. Love bears all things and does not self-select which aspects of someone should be loved. Love believes all things, as its intentions are pure. Love hopes for all things, as true love has no limits. Love endures all things and does not walk away during times of adversity.

God is clear—love is the greatest task we face, and it is not about saying the word but acting upon it. In a real sense, love is an action word and when you have experienced love the word is always supported by tangible acts. Today interrogate the love that surrounds you and ask yourself if you are being fed empty words and promises or the love that God intends. If you determine you have people in your life who truly love you, then it is imperative to be thankful to God. But if you discover there are some who are imposters of love, you must love them some more. Loving those who love you is a simple task. But the blessing or reward comes when you learn to love your enemies. I love you despite your anger, envy, arrogance, boastful nature, pride, selfishness, lies, and the pain I have allowed you to cause. I love you because God instructs me to love those who hate me. But He never stated I needed to stay with you. Today I say goodbye to the imposter of love and will seek those who are capable of loving me as God intends.

FEAR NOT

The Lord is with me; I will not be afraid. What can people do to me?   Psalm 118:6 ISV

For God did not give us a spirit of timidity, but a spirit of power, of love and of self-discipline.   2 Timothy 1:7 ISV

> There is no fear in love. But perfect love drives out fear, because
> fear has to do with punishment. The one who fears is not made
> perfect in love.   1 John 4:18

As Christians, we express our love for God and the miraculous gift of His son Jesus, but many of us are tormented by our fear of the unknown. We are more than familiar with the scriptures, which tell us not to fear, as the Lord is with us always. We understand we are not called to be fearful, and we further acknowledge how our fear gives Satan room to attack us while we are afraid. Nonetheless, as a child is fearful of the monsters under his or her bed because of their elusive imagination, we too struggle with fear. Despite our continual encouragement, a child still struggles with the darkness of night, monsters who reside under his or her bed, and the thunderstorms that torment the sky. Only when a child begins to wrestle with reality and learn that the greatest monster of them all is fear, can they find rest. Unfortunately, just like children, we magnify our fears and not our God. But we too must realize He is so much bigger than our fears.

The Bible says, "Come," he said. Then Peter got down out of the boat, walked on the water, and came toward Jesus. But when he saw the wind, he was afraid and, beginning to sink, cried out, "Lord, save me!" (Matthew 14:29-30). God is asking us to walk and not be distracted by the circumstances of our lives, for the moment we lose focus and succumb to fear, we will drown in our sorrow. Today we must stop punishing ourselves with fear and boldly face our situations. God has the ability to move through the storm with you. Just like He was with the Hebrew boys, He will stand in the fire with you, and through His miraculous power make you fireproof.

No longer will I be a prisoner of my fear, for God is with me, and He will break every chain the enemy has placed upon me. Today I can finally walk in my freedom, understanding that man has no power. I once was a slave to fear and Satan attempted to destroy my destiny. Oh but God rose up in me and I knew the battle was over for sickness, pain, death, financial ruin, betrayal, divorce, wayward children, corruption, envy, immorality. All these schemes of the enemy were minuscule compared to the power of God. Today I have my swagger back and boldly tell Satan to get behind me, for the Lord is my protector. Whom should I fear?

WAIT WITH EXPECTANCY

Let us not become weary in doing good, for at the proper time we will reap a harvest if we do not give up.   Galatians 6:9

I waited patiently for the Lord; he turned to me and heard my cry.   Psalm 40:1

Blessed is the one who perseveres under trial because, having stood the test, that person will receive the crown of life that the Lord has promised to those who love him.   James 1:12

Brothers and sisters, I do not consider myself yet to have taken hold of it. But one thing I do: Forgetting what is behind and straining toward what is ahead, I press on toward the goal to win the prize for which God has called me heavenward in Christ Jesus.   Philippians 3:13-14

The Bible is equipped with numerous scriptures about waiting. Yet many of us struggle during the waiting season. We live in a time where we have become accustomed to instant gratification. The advancements in technology, information gathering, social media and other forms of access enable our desire to constantly pacify our need for instant fulfillment, which, unfortunately, hinders our ability to wait on the Lord. Most Americans love dogs, as they represent a sense of loyalty and obedience. A well-trained dog is impressive. It knows to sit at an intersection, not to sit on the furniture, and to stop when its owner gives the command. But what is most impressive is their exhilaration as their owner returns home. As humans, we proudly understand we are the most advanced living species known to man, as our ability to think, rationalize, and express emotion is far more complex than any other living organism. However, a dog understands their existence is contingent on their master's ability to protect them and provide them with the necessities of life like food, water, shelter, and love. Unfortunately, there are dog owners who are abusive. But even in those cases, the dog's loyalty and obedience typically does not waver as it waits for its owner to return home.

We serve a God who is incapable of not loving us. He is never abusive nor lacking in His ability to provide for us, but we must learn to wait on Him. In a real sense, God has us in our current situation not as punishment but as a means for preparation for what is to come. Our struggle rests in our anxiety and impatience. But we must understand that if God has you in a situation, He can bless you in the midst of the storm. Today if your prayer has been to escape from the darkness of your situation, it is time you look toward God. You desire to escape, and He is keeping you there only because there is a blessing within your surroundings. Our reward comes from our ability to wait and know that God hears our cry and is preparing our harvest. Stand by the door, run to the windows, shout uncontrollably, and run in circles because God is about to reward your waiting. Get ready, for He has a blessing with your name on it!

HUMILITY IN TRAGEDY, TRUTH, AND TRIUMPH

Do nothing out of selfish ambition or vain conceit. Rather, in humility value others above yourselves, not looking to your own interests but each of you to the interests of the others. In your relationships with one another, have the same mindset as Christ Jesus: Philippians 2:3-5

But he gives more grace. Therefore it says, "God opposes the proud, but gives grace to the humble."   James 4:6 ESV

Whoever exalts himself will be humbled, and whoever humbles himself will be exalted.   Matthew 23:12 ESV

We live in a world fueled by competitiveness, individualism, and meritocracy. As a result, many of us operate as a team of me, only supporting our self-interests. While many of us boast about our affinity for collaboration during interviews or social gatherings, our actions represent a commitment solely to ourselves. When engaging in dialog, our conversations are often self-centered, focusing on our accomplishments and career goals. They inherently lack authenticity, as they are submerged in superficial notions. As Christians, our legacy is our commitment to the plan and purpose of God, and it is bigger than stock portfolios, educational attainment, our home, or the cars we drive.

God has called us to be humble, not arrogant. Even the most successful person has to face death, tragedy, loss, and disappointment. The world would have you believe that success is tied to material things, but it is a fallacy. When you pass away, someone else will sleep in your bed, wear your clothes, and live without your physical presence. Humility allows you to understand that there is something greater than your own interest; that something is God.

We must have humility in tragedy, truth, and triumph. If you have lost a loved one, do not make it about yourself. Make it about God. If you know something to be true, use it to help others as opposed to using it to help yourself. If you have won a victory, allow your celebration to build up others and not yourself. Jesus humbled himself and died on the cross. He allowed himself to be humiliated for our transgressions. Jesus would often introduce himself by saying, "I am who I say I am," not providing a resume of his miracles, the places he has traveled, or a financial report of his assets.

Today humble yourself. Stop talking with vain conceit. Stop trying to become someone you are not. Stop seeking validation from the world. Stop doing the same things repeatedly, and start having the attitude of Christ Jesus. A true king never has to state their authority or kingship, but simply can say I am. Your decision is clear, you can choose to live a life of humility, or God will humble you.

PEACE BEYOND OUR UNDERSTANDING: PRICELESS

For God is not a God of disorder but of peace—as in all the congregations of the Lord's people.   1 Corinthians 14:33

"Come to me, all you who are weary and burdened, and I will give you rest. Take my yoke upon you and learn from me, for I am gentle and humble in heart, and you will find rest for your souls. For my yoke is easy and my burden is light."   Matthew 11:28-30

The Lord gives strength to his people; the Lord blesses his people with peace.   Psalm 29:11

Though the mountains be shaken and the hills be removed, yet my unfailing love for you will not be shaken nor my covenant of peace be removed," says the Lord, who has compassion on you.
                                                        Isaiah 54:10

Life is filled with many transitions that cause our moods to shift and our peace to become compromised. Whether you are in the office or in the comfort of your home, it seems our peace is continually under attack. The reality is that peace comes directly from God, and the enemy is disturbed when you choose to live in peace. How many times have you been watching your favorite reality show and said to yourself, "These people are dysfunctional"? Hollywood has made a fortune by exposing the inherent craziness in the lives of others. But as we watch intensely, we simultaneously forget the turmoil we ourselves have decided to deal with every day. For the record, arguing, fighting, anxiety, abuse, lack of structure, disorder, unstable finances, poor decisions, gossip, blameworthiness, envy, and many other frailties in our lives create a space for dysfunction, which disrupts peace. Clearly God demands a certain work environment, which is void of disorder. If we would learn to take our issues to the Lord and not to substance abuse or some other temporal fix that we believe relives the pain, then we would have peace.

The greatness of God is that He can give you peace in your brokenness if you decide to come to Him. Today, the mountains have been shaken, and the hills have fallen but God is still on the throne, and He will not be moved. God does not have the luxury of shutting down but is always working for those who love Him. You must make a conscious decision to live in peace, for if you allow the enemy to rob you of this gift, you will feel like a wanderer in a foreign land. Do not allow the enemy to win, but believe in God to grant you peace that is beyond your understanding. Through all the storms of life, stand firmly rooted in God's love and perfect peace, and He will deliver. Tell the enemy your peace is not for sale, for it is simply priceless.

CORRECTION, NOT JUDGMENT

You, therefore, have no excuse, you who pass judgment on someone else, for at whatever point you judge another, you are condemning yourself because you who pass judgment do the same things. Now we know that God's judgment against those who do such things is based on truth. So when you, a mere man, pass judgment on them and yet do the same things, do you think you will escape God's judgment? Or do you show contempt for the riches of his kindness, forbearance, and patience, not realizing that God's kindness is intended to lead you to repentance?   Romans 2:1-4

"Do not judge, or you too will be judged. For in the same way you judge others, you will be judged, and with the measure you use, it will be measured to you."   Matthew 7:1-2

One thing most of us can agree upon is that we live in a world of rules and regulations. It is rare that someone will question the importance of allowing one person to speak at a time, as the contrary will cause disorder and chaos. If someone blatantly runs a red light, we are not quick to justify their actions but likely discern their actions are against the traffic safety rules. Furthermore, we live in a nation that has a judicial system comprised of judges, attorneys, defendants, plaintiffs, and jurors who convene in a courtroom to render judgment.

In a perfect world, all criminals would be charged, and all innocent people would be acquitted. But this is not the case. We have heard of countless cases where people have served decades for a crime that they did not commit, as DNA evidence proved their innocence. The inherent corruption within the penal system is not a new occurrence. Cases dating back to the early 1900's have proven to be a legal debacle. These realities are predicated on many social inequalities, ranging from race to gender, but overall we believe the judicial system works.

An important component of the judicial system is the presenting of the facts. Well if we step outside of the courtroom and into our personal lives, we too operate as the all-encompassing judge, but often we render a judgment with little to no facts and no proven authority. Jesus serves as an example of a wrongfully convicted person, as the guilty Barabbas was released while Jesus was sentenced to death. Jesus stood before a crowd of his peers and the charges where stated. With a resounding voice, his peers yelled, "Crucify him."

We are quick to see the injustice in the penal system as it relates to high profile cases like O.J. Simpson or Casey Anthony, but we are hesitant to convict ourselves for passing judgment on others. The Bible is clear that we are not to judge others, as oftentimes our opinions are not rooted in truth. How can the adulterer judge the fornicator? How can the thief judge the liar? How can the jealous one judge success? How can the gossiper judge the betrayer? And really how can the sinner judge the sinner? However, there is a distinct difference between judgment and correction. If someone who loves the Lord tells you something about yourself which is aligned with God's principles, then do not foolishly mistake their gentle correction for judgment. If a child were to run in the middle of a busy intersection, would you say, "Let me not say anything because I do not want to judge" or would you immediately move to correct the ill-fated behavior of the child? As Christians, we must help each other stay on the narrow road to salvation, or we will all perish for our lack of wisdom.

Today let us not judge, for as the Bible states, we will be judged by the same measure. However, we must welcome correction, as it allows us to become better people. Those who are hesitant to change are quick to confuse correction with judgment. In those cases where you feel you are being judged, ask yourself if there is any truth in the accusation. For example, if you are, in fact, an alcoholic and a thief tells you to stop drinking, what will be your response? "How are you going to tell me to stop drinking and you break into people's homes? At least I am only hurting myself." Or will you say, "Although I feel you are judging me, what you are saying is true. I will continue to overcome my addiction, and I will pray for you. Thank you for your concern."

We must understand that God will judge us all. Our role is not to ridicule others or pass judgment about the actions of others, but to gently correct those who are in need. The only way we can help each other is through correction, not judgment.

You, therefore, have no excuse, you who pass judgment on someone else, for at whatever point you judge another, you are condemning yourself, because you who pass judgment do the same things. Now we know that God's judgment against those who do such things is based on truth. So when you, a mere human being, pass judgment on them and yet do the same things, do you think you will escape God's judgment? Or do you show contempt for the riches of his kindness, forbearance and patience, not realizing that God's kindness is intended to lead you to repentance? Romans 2:1-4

REFLECTION 4

GOD'S FAVOR SILENCES THE ENEMY

Surely, Lord, you bless the righteous; you surround them with your favor as with a shield.   Psalm 5:12

May the favor of the Lord our God rest on us; establish the work of our hands for us—yes, establish the work of our hands.

Psalm 90:17

For the Lord God is a sun and shield; the Lord bestows favor and honor; no good thing does he withhold from those whose walk is blameless.   Psalm 84:11

In him we have obtained an inheritance, having been predestined according to the purpose of him who works all things according to the counsel of his will.   Ephesians 1:11 ESV

It is time for us to be honest and let the world know our success has never solely been correlated to our talents or abilities. In a real sense, our greatest asset to success has been the favor of God. There are many people who believe in serendipity, which means a fortunate mistake, and there are others who believe in luck, which is based on chance. However, these ideologies have proven to fail over time. At some point, you will feel the unfortunate nature of your mistakes and luck will simply run out. God has promised to provide favor to those who are righteous. He will operate as a shield of protection.

If we are willing to work, God will enhance our limited ability and increase our reward through favor. He will not withhold anything from those who serve him. Did God withhold miracles from Moses? Did God withhold a son from Abraham? Did God withhold protection from Noah? Did God withhold resurrection from Jesus? Then why would He withhold His blessings from you?

The enemy is not impressed with our talent and believes that if he can minimize our ability, he can destroy our destiny. However, our strength is not based on the world's concept of success. Take away my home and all my worldly possessions, and the enemy will learn that my favor is greater than all the riches of the world. God allowed you to take my home, but He has blessed me with a new one. You had to take public transportation, but now you own your vehicle. You quit your job of more than twenty years, but now you run your own company because God's favor is beyond our understanding. I did not apply for a particular job, but I received an offer. I was not qualified for a particular position, but I was promoted. I am not worthy, but He continues to bless my life. Today, we must realize favor seems to be unfair only to those who do not understand the love of God. Your credentials are minuscule compared to God's promises. The Bible says in Him we have gained an inheritance. Well, today is your day to claim what has been bequeathed to you, and that is simply the favor of God. He has a blessing with your name on it, and no one has the authority to claim what is rightfully yours. Take possession of what God has promised. He has divinely placed you in the position of greatness. For those who need or demand a reason for your success, simply silence them by saying, "God's favor."

FROM DEATH VALLEY TO THE MOUNTAINTOP: FOUR STAGES OF LIFE

Even though I walk through the valley of the shadow of death, I will fear no evil, for you are with me; your rod and your staff, they comfort me.   Psalm 23:4 ESV

I will lift up my eyes to the hills—From whence comes my help? My help comes from the Lord, Who made heaven and earth.
Psalm 121:1-2 NKJV

Have I not commanded you? Be strong and courageous. Do not be frightened, and do not be dismayed, for the Lord your God is with you wherever you go.   Joshua 1:9 ESV

According to Webster's dictionary, a valley is a low period, point, or level. A plain is a large area of flat land without trees. A hill is usually a rounded area of land that is higher than the land around it, but that is not as high as a mountain. A mountain is an area of land that rises very high above the land around it and is higher than a hill.

There are four distinct stages of life, which produce various emotions and can operate as obstacles if we are not careful. The two most often talked about stages are our valley and mountaintop experiences. People seem eager to rest in the victim mentality of the valley. How often have you heard people say, "I'm going through"? Another common phrase that people say is, "If it isn't one thing, it's another." For some, these are sure signs of a valley experience. But their cry is not for prayer. It is for attention. In a real sense, we are all going through something. However, those who are deeply rooted in God are less likely to complain or bring attention to their circumstance, but rest in knowing that God walks with them through their valley experience. Perhaps they reflect on the Hebrew boys or the crucifixion as a reminder that, because God is with us always and will stand in the fire with us, there is no need for pity or complaining. Some of the people who are dealing with the most trying situations are those who do not place their pain on stage, but take their burdens to Christ. We too must eliminate the inherent negativity of the valley experience. If we allow God to reign in our lives, we can rewrite the statement and say, "God continues to bless us in spite of our circumstances."

Some people feel as though their life is set on a plain, as it lacks growth but is void of the gurgling realities of the valley. It is imperative you do not find contentment in your "plain" experience, but trust that God is preparing you for the next big thing. Unfortunately, many people spend an immense amount of time looking down and finding joy that their situation is not as daunting as the valley experience. But this is a gross waste of time. It becomes vital for you to focus on the hill, for it gives you the motivation to rise above your stagnate place.

Then, there are those who are living on the hill, but spending too much time looking downward. When you have reached the stage of the hill, you sometimes might feel that you have arrived. Things that used to be an issue are no longer an obstacle. The sad reality about the hilltop is that those who are not careful fall rapidly back down to the valley. Failure to submit to God at your highest point forces you to submit to Him at your lowest point. As you begin to ascend, it becomes imperative to pray, as the enemy finds joy in knocking you down from your position of greatness.

Lastly, the mountain experience allows us to stand at the highest elevation and look out over the land, knowing that God has placed us in a position of prominence. Today stand in whatever stage you are currently in, for God delivers, and you will walk into your destiny. Do not spend your time looking down but look to the hills and even past the mountains, for God is ready to take you higher. Be bold and say, "God has taken me from Death Valley to the Mountaintop."

A WOUNDED WARRIOR: A TESTIMONY OF SCARS

"You are a king, then!" said Pilate. Jesus answered, "You say that I am a king. In fact, the reason I was born and came into the world is to testify to the truth. Everyone on the side of truth listens to me."   John 18:37

"You would have no power over me if it were not given to you from above. Therefore the one who handed me over to you is guilty of a greater sin."   John 19:11

When he had received the drink, Jesus said, "It is finished." With that he bowed his head and gave up his spirit.   John 19:30

"Look at my hands and my feet. It is I myself! Touch me and see;
a ghost does not have flesh and bones, as you see I have."

Luke 24:39

The story of the crucifixion is one of the most retold accounts of the
Bible, for it chronicles the grueling final hours of Jesus Christ. In addition, it serves as the greatest testimony of Jesus. Although the world
questioned if Jesus was the King of the Jews, He never gave in to the
opinions of the world but was confident and trusted His Father. Jesus
was arrested and interrogated by Pilate. His conversations with Pilate
were fascinating, as Pilate knew that He was an innocent man but ultimately conceded to the demands of the crowd. Jesus was tried by his
peers and sentenced to death. Prior to being nailed to the cross, Jesus
had been severely beaten, and His flesh was torn from His body. While
on the cross, His side was pierced by one of the guards. It is fair to say
that Jesus was wounded.

The crowds mocked Him, as they believed Caesar was the only king.
The wounded King would soon succumb to the brutality of the enemy, but died knowing that His Father would fulfill His promise. The
scripture says He gave up His spirit, which implies that Jesus had the
full authority to come down from the cross. Jesus understood that no
weapon formed by the enemy prospers. On the third day, Jesus was
resurrected, and His wounds became scars. His scars proved to His
doubting disciples that He had risen.

Today we must decide to represent our scars and not our wounds.

Wounds force you to blame others and live in a constant state of pain, but scars allow you to reflect on endurance, healing, and victory. Jesus allowed His enemy to wound Him, for He knew the pain of the wounds was small compared to what His scars would represent. Do you have wounds of abandonment, physical or sexual abuse, rejection, insecurity, blame, failure, or something that keeps you in a constant state of emotional or physical pain? If so, it is time to heal from your wounds. We have all been wounded, but with God we always have victory. The world will continually stare at your scars and will try to make you insecure. But say to them, "I once was a wounded warrior only noticed by my pain, but now I have a testimony of scars."

FOOLISH AMBITION: A MISSION OF DISAPPOINTMENT

For what does it profit a man if he gains the whole world and loses or forfeits himself?   Luke 9:25 ESV

What causes quarrels and what causes fights among you? Is it not this, that your passions are at war within you? You desire and do not have, so you murder. You covet and cannot obtain, so you fight and quarrel. You do not have, because you do not ask.

James 4:1-2 ESV

For all that is in the world—the desires of the flesh and the desires of the eyes and pride of life—is not from the Father but is from the world.   1 John 2:16 ESV

We live in a society fueled by competition, meritocracy, and prosperity. But the Bible offers an interesting perspective about ambition. For clarity, the Bible speaks about those who are rich and seems to indicate that their life can be clouded by their wealth. However, to assume all people with wealth are ill-fated is a mistake.

Each of us operates with an internal drive for success, but the difference lies in how we pursue our dreams. Unfortunately, reality television and the media have heavily influenced our ambition. After watching your favorite reality television show, you will see countless images of designer handbags, luxury cars, massive mansions, and other extravagant things. Beyond the glamor is a human being who has to deal with the complexities of life irrespective of their financial status.

The late Michael Jackson wanted to become the biggest touring artist of all time, but his ambition was halted by his premature death. Jackson is considered a music icon, but with all his fame and fortune, he could not escape the complexities of life. With a cardiologist by his bedside, Michael Jackson died on June 25, 2009. The late Steve Jobs is considered a world leader in innovation, as he changed how we buy, sell, and listen to music. That is coupled with his contributions on a grander scale to technology. Yet, Jobs had a rare form of cancer and died on October 5, 2011 after a tumultuous battle with the disease. Despite his ambition, perfectionism, and his multi-billion dollar fortune, he too had to endure the complexities of life.

The average person might not think there are any similarities between a billionaire and a person of lower economic status, but they would be mistaken. Whether you are rich or poor, you will have to contend with life and no matter how many earthly possessions you acquire, you cannot escape the inherent difficulties of life. Ambition is great, for it represents your passion. But if your passion is not rooted in God, your ambition will leave you disappointed. Today ask yourself what is the foundation of your ambition. Is it greed, insecurity, arrogance, invincibility, or God? Greed is for those who continue to want more, despite already having an abundance. Insecurity is for those who foolishly believe that if they succeed, it will change their opinion of themselves. But money cannot purchase true confidence, for it only pacifies it. Arrogance is for those who believe their success gives them authority, which creates a false sense of power. Invincibility is for those who believe their success exempts them from the disappointments of life. But such a notion is simply unrealistic.

However, when God is the foundation of your ambition you understand that your success is not solely intended for personal gain but to serve others. Furthermore, it is important to dream and to have ambition for great things, but we must not seek riches at the expense of losing ourselves. Ask yourself why you want them so badly. Allow God to be the center of your being and chase those things which He has placed in your heart, not the selfish desires of the world. When you have foolish ambition, it will lead to a mission of disappointment.

A CONSTANT STATE OF THANKFULNESS

I always thank my God for you because of his grace given you in Christ Jesus. For in him you have been enriched in every way— with all kinds of speech and all knowledge.   1 Corinthians 1:4-5

All this is for your benefit, so that the grace that is reaching more and more people may cause thanksgiving to overflow to the glory of God. Therefore we do not lose heart. Though outwardly we are wasting away, yet inwardly we are being renewed day by day.

2 Corinthians 4:15-16

Give thanks in all circumstances, for this is God's will for you in Christ Jesus.   1 Thessalonians 5:18

Each year as the holidays approach, families across the nation give thanks for their many blessings. But thankfulness should not be an annual ritual. The Bible instructs us to be thankful daily and for all of our circumstances. It is easy to be thankful as you sit before a feast, have shelter, clothes, warmth, and comfort. But what about those who are homeless or simply without the common necessities of life? It is baffling and sickening that some of us notice the homeless community only during the holiday season, but these same people are struggling throughout the year. We rationalize our behavior by believing they are in their situation because of poor decisions, mental illness, or perhaps their innate laziness. But even if our sentiments were correct, we are certainly in a position to feed a homeless person.

For those organizations that are committed to the cause of eradicating homelessness, we applaud your efforts. But as Christ's followers, we have a moral obligation to be concerned about the state of humanity. The late Dr. King said, "Life's most persistent and urgent question is what are you doing for others?" The sinful and shameful reality is that we treat the homeless community as if they are invisible. Whether you are in the park in Philadelphia, the magnificent mile in Chicago or in the nation's capital, homelessness is a constant reality. It should not be ignored.

The irony of it all is that many people of the homeless community arise every single morning thanking God, not for their lavish lifestyle, but for their survival. God's grace is sufficient and in Him we are rich in every way, for Christ died for the benefit of humanity. Whether you are in a penthouse or living on the streets of Brooklyn, give thanks. Whether you have succeeded or failed, give thanks. Whether you are healthy or sick, give thanks. Whether you are young or old, give thanks. Whether you are rich or poor, give thanks. Whether you are highly educated or a high school dropout, give thanks, for the Bible says give thanks in all circumstances.

Today serve others as God instructs us. Above all things, love your brother as you would love yourself. We are all brothers and sisters in Christ, seeking the kingdom of heaven. There, no one will be forgotten or pitied, but we all will be filled with the abundant blessings and favor of our Father. There is no reason for us to be unthankful. We must learn to live in a constant state of thankfulness, for God is more than enough.

THE POWER OF RECONCILIATION

When Joseph's brothers saw that their father was dead, they said, "What if Joseph holds a grudge against us and pays us back for all the wrongs we did to him?" So they sent word to Joseph, saying, "Your father left these instructions before he died: 'This is what you are to say to Joseph: I ask you to forgive your brothers the sins and the wrongs they committed in treating you so badly.' Now please forgive the sins of the servants of the God of your father." When their message came to him, Joseph wept. His brothers then came and threw themselves down before him. "We are your slaves," they said. But Joseph said to them, "Don't be afraid. Am I in the place of God? You intended to harm me, but God intended it for good to accomplish what is now being done, the saving of many lives. So then, don't be afraid. I will provide for you and your children." And he reassured them and spoke kindly to them.

Genesis 50:15-21

We are therefore Christ's ambassadors, as though God were making his appeal through us. We implore you on Christ's behalf: Be reconciled to God. God made him who had no sin to be sin for us, so that in him we might become the righteousness of God.

2 Corinthians 5:20-21

Joseph's brothers initially plotted to kill him but decided that selling him into Egypt would be more beneficial for them. When they returned home, they explained to their father Jacob that a ferocious animal had attacked Joseph. They then showed their father Joseph's severely torn robe, which had been dipped in blood.

It is written that Joseph later ascended to power based on Pharaoh's order to place him in charge of Egypt. His brothers went to Egypt to purchase food during a famine but did not recognize their brother. Joseph eventually revealed himself to his brothers, and they were terrified he would have them killed. The brothers wanted Joseph's forgiveness to reconcile their relationship.

Joseph forgave them for their schemes, as he understood that while their mission was to bring harm to him, God used their wickedness to bless others. Joseph understood his purpose in life was not to be merciless like his brothers or live with a burning hatred, but to have a reconciled heart.

Today you must seek reconciliation and not allow the enemy to win by having resentment towards those who intended harm. To the father who walked out, it is reconciled. To the mother who knowingly allowed her children to be victims of molestation, it is reconciled. To the boss who manipulated the facts and caused you to lose your job, it is reconciled. To the jealous friend, it is reconciled. To the adulterous spouse, it is reconciled. To all those who intend harm, it is reconciled. The enemy has absolutely no power and will have to crawl to your feet, as God will place you in a position of authority only because He knows your response to their evilness will be love. How could I not love those who are responsible for my promotion and rise to greatness? God's favor is exemplified through the power of reconciliation.

Learning to Live Life on a Budget

"For which of you, desiring to build a tower, does not first sit down and count the cost, whether he has enough to complete it?"

Luke 14:28 ESV

A wise man thinks ahead; a fool doesn't, and even brags about it!

Proverbs 13:16 LB

The rich rules over the poor, and the borrower becomes the lender's slave.

Proverbs 22:7 NASB

The Lord will open for you His good treasury, the heavens, to give rain to your land in its season and to bless all the work of your hand; and you shall lend to many nations, but you shall not borrow.   Deuteronomy 28:12 ESV

Many years ago, it seemed to be the standard to live on a budget and to minimize excess spending in effort to maximize cash flow. Thus, families were inclined to save before making a big purchase, like buying an automobile or home. But it is different today. Some people are content with financing their desires, even though they do not have the ability to pay for them outright. Other people lack adequate financial resources and simply have more expenses than income. Unfortunately, there are countless others who live from paycheck to paycheck. They often attribute their financial woes with not having enough money but refuse to be accountable for their poor spending habits.

Society is partly to blame for creating a system of consumerism and materialism through the means of advertising. Also, our obsession with the rich and famous can distort our ability to be rational in our spending habits. Reality television places a high premium on financial success. But if you watch carefully, even the rich and famous struggle to live within their financial means.

It would be unfair to blame society alone for our financial irresponsibility, as we have agency to fight against consumerism. When you are at the kiosk or tech store, you have the power to decide that your current computer or smartphone is sufficient. But often you swipe your credit card and allow yourself to be a product of materialism, which can cause a financial crisis. Parents often find themselves buying their children all of the latest gadgets and things they desire. But this behavior will only gain temporal happiness for the child while placing the family in financial turmoil.

For parents who are affluent, it is equally important to live on a budget as a means to teach your children financial responsibility. Failure to do so will make your children feel a sense of entitlement. To love your child or to be considered a good parent does not mean that you must give them all they want at the expense of causing your family financial ruin. Today should be the day when you sit down, count the cost, be wise, and think ahead. The smartphone, designer clothes, or extravagant birthday parties for a toddler will not pay for the rising cost of college, nor will it gain compounded interest like a mutual fund.

In a real sense, you have become content with being a borrower, but God instructs us to be lenders and not slaves to debt. It makes absolutely no sense to have on designer attire and a bank account in the red. If you are sporting a thousand-dollar handbag but cannot make the minimum credit card payment perhaps, you should not have purchased it. Learn to stay in your financial lane. Learn to live life on a budget.

MOVING FROM PAIN TO PURPOSE

Beloved, do not be surprised at the fiery trial when it comes upon you to test you, as though something strange were happening to you. But rejoice insofar as you share Christ's sufferings, that you may also rejoice and be glad when his glory is revealed.

1 Peter 4:12-13 ESV

Finally, brothers, whatever is true, whatever is honorable, whatever is just, whatever is pure, whatever is lovely, whatever is commendable, if there is any excellence, if there is anything worthy of praise, think about these things.   Philippians 4:8 ESV

Archie Manning is the father of Cooper, Peyton, and Eli. Archie was considered a premier athlete, as he was sought after by Major League Baseball and the NFL. But his rise to fame began as starting quarterback for Ole Miss. His talent was unparalleled at the time. He had an ability to run the football as a quarterback like no one else and scored many touchdowns.

At the height of his career, he went home to discover his father had committed suicide. He was willing to give up his college career to support his mother and sister, but his family encouraged him to return to school. After his father's death, his accomplishments were remarkable. But some would argue his greatest accomplishment of all was being an active father to his three children.

He never pressured his sons to play football, but naturally they wanted to be like their dad. Archie was the king of home videos and had countless hours of footage of the boys playing football in the backyard. To this day, his sons praise their dad for being a loving father, as they really did not understand the magnitude of his fame during their youth.

Cooper, the oldest son, was considered a great receiver and had great prospects for college, but was diagnosed with spinal stenosis, which ended his ability to play football. Peyton vowed to play for his brother, as his dad was heartbroken that his son Cooper could not live out his dreams. Peyton would become a nationally-ranked college athlete and later go to the NFL. Lastly, there was Eli, who would attend Ole Miss, break the records of his father, and later play in the NFL.

Collectively the Manning family has received numerous trophies and broken many records but, above all, the glory is a father who loved his three sons. Archie's wife Olivia is proud of her children, but marvels at the life they have been afforded. She says she is humbled by it all.

Today is the day you must not wallow in your pain, but find the strength to press forward. Life is about choices. What would have happened if Archie had stayed home after his father's death? He would not have met Olivia, and there would be no Cooper, Peyton, or Eli. Sometimes our destiny is wrapped in our pain but we fail to take hold of the glory which will be revealed. Archie had every right to be bitter but chose to focus on what was pure, which was the love of his children. God loves us and desires to move us from pain to purpose. But we must hold on.

BORN TO BECOME

The Word became flesh and made his dwelling among us. We have seen his glory, the glory of the one and only, who came from the Father, full of grace and truth.   John 1:14

Since the beginning of time, we have celebrated birth and mourned death, but the birth of Jesus is notably the greatest of all. It is written that He was born in a manger and entered the world not as royalty but exemplifying humility. Most of us can say we were born in the convenience of a hospital. Not Jesus. During the holiday season, we must not forget the greatest gift given to humanity: the birth, death, and resurrection of Jesus the Christ.

The agnostic believes there is something greater than the human species but does not claim it is God. The atheist believes such talk of a supreme creator is preposterous and boldly claims God does not exist. Many religious faiths argue over if Jesus is the Messiah. The evolutionist believes the human species evolved over many years and touts its scientific analysis to prove its theory. The historian argues that the Bible has a storyline that is not factually accurate and is an adaptation of previous works. The cynic argues that since man is the author of the Bible, it is incapable of being accurate.

As humans, we seem inclined to argue about our beliefs but our persuasive tactics have not rendered universal consensus. We will likely continue to debate the existence of God, and thus the birth of His son Jesus. For those who believe in Jesus, there is no question He was born to Mary and Joseph. It can be easy to become sidetracked by the debate and miss the message. Unless you are like Enoch or Elijah, it is a safe assertion to state that those who are born will eventually die. Therefore, our primary concern is to understand why we were born and for what purpose.

Similar to the birth of Jesus, there is inherent confusion and controversy surrounding many of us as we grapple with the complexities of life. For example, why are children dying of leukemia and other diseases? Why are children being gunned down in their schools? Why would a world rich in resources allow people to die of starvation? Why do we question the truth but embrace untruths? The answers lie in our ability to know that we are limited in our understanding.

Today we must understand that just like Jesus, we were born to be great. He went from a baby born in a manger, to an adolescent child, to a man nailed to a cross, and to a Savior that has risen. What is your life's trajectory? Why were you born? The answer is that you were simply born to become.

A NEW BEGINNING CAN START TODAY

For I know the plans I have for you, declares the Lord, plans for welfare and not for evil, to give you a future and a hope.

Jeremiah 29:11 ESV

Remember not the former things, nor consider the things of old. Behold, I am doing a new thing; now it springs forth, do you not perceive it? I will make a way in the wilderness and rivers in the desert. Isaiah 43:18-19 ESV

The steadfast love of the Lord never ceases; his mercies never come to an end; they are new every morning; great is your faithfulness. "The Lord is my portion," says my soul, "therefore I will hope in him." Lamentations 3:22-24 ESV

As each new year rapidly approaches, many people will make resolutions ranging from being more health conscious to being more responsible with their finances. Health clubs are elated about this time of year, as they see a spike in membership sales. Bankers have an influx of customers looking for ways to invest money. Some people return to the church. Unfortunately, these common resolutions are often not maintained over the long haul, as people waver in their commitment.

With great excitement, millions of people around the world celebrate the New Year. But once the clock strikes midnight and the fireworks have ended, we must face the realities of the present moment. The clichéd statements of "time is moving fast" or "it's the New Year already" do little to account for the many missed opportunities of maximizing our time. Setting goals and resolutions is admirable, but you must have tenacity to achieve your aspirations. It is important to set realistic goals, as failure to do so will lead to disappointment.

Change is often difficult when you procrastinate, have unhealthy habits, display complacency, do things as a means of compliance, or surround yourself with people who encourage your bad behavior. The Bible says God has plans for us. But those plans are easily halted when we fail to change. God is awesome and instructs us to move beyond the former, focusing on the new thing that God intends for our lives. His ability is not compromised by our current circumstances, but we must allow Him to become our flowing river in the desert.

Every morning we are blessed with a new set of mercies and must be willing to embrace change. Regardless of whether today is the New

Year or not, it is the perfect day for you to change. Change is difficult. Just ask the heart patient who has to change their lifestyle drastically or the junk food junky who has been diagnosed with diabetes. Although change is difficult, it has to be done if you desire to become a better you. Make no excuses and hold no grudges. Decide to change today, as the time for change is always now. Trust in the Lord at all times and unequivocally know that a new beginning can start today.

For I know the plans I have for you, declares the Lord, plans for welfare and not for evil, to give you a future and a hope.   *Jeremiah 29:11ESV*

REFLECTION 5

ONE TRUE FRIENDSHIP LEADS TO GREATER RELATIONSHIPS

A man of many companions may come to ruin, but there is a friend who sticks closer than a brother.   Proverbs 18:24 ESV

Do not be deceived: "Bad company ruins good morals."
                                        1 Corinthians 15:33 ESV

Two are better than one, because they have a good reward for their toil. For if they fall, one will lift up his fellow. But woe to him who is alone when he falls and has not another to lift him up! Again, if two lie together, they keep warm, but how can one keep warm alone? And though a man might prevail against one who is alone, two will withstand him—a threefold cord is not quickly broken.
                                        Ecclesiastes 4:9-12 ESV

Greater love has no one than this, that someone lay down his life for his friends.   John 15:13 ESV

Through socialization, children quickly learn the importance of so-cial interaction and friendships. When preschoolers return home from their daily activities and discuss their day, it often includes talking about their friends. As parents, we are excited that our child's behavior displays a healthy emotional balance. If suddenly our child's behavior changes, we instinctively question their relationships to discern if their new behavior is a result of emulating a friend. As parents, we are in total agreement with the biblical teaching that instructs us to rid ourselves of bad company in an effort to not compromise our judgment or morals. When children become older, their friendship pool dwindles as they begin to understand the need to have quality and not quantity in their friendships. In adulthood, given that we have grown from our childhood ideology and become committed to our Christian faith, we unequivocally understand that the greatest relationship of all is the one we have developed with Christ.

The Bible is clear and supports quality relationships, but we must grasp the entire facts about friendship. First, do not be consumed by having a lot of people around you who are not really your friends. Second, if someone is a true friend, your combined efforts will be greater than your individual talents. A friend is loyal and is not jealous or envious of your success or talent but is overjoyed by all of your accomplishments. A friend will be your encouragement in times of failure and your cheerleader in times of victory. Third, even your best friend over time will hurt you and perhaps even disappoint you, but they will work tirelessly for your forgiveness. A friend adheres to your needs and changes without being forced, as they are constantly considering your feelings. Your friendship should continually grow and become stronger. Last, the greatest friend of all is Jesus.

Today it is important that you analyze your friendships and end those that are unproductive and toxic. It is foolish to believe that as humans we were created to be without companionship. But what is even more foolish is to create relationships that compromise our integrity. If you are partnered with someone who makes you feel uneasy or they take you to a place where you cannot recognize yourself, chances are you are in a bad relationship.

The popular reality television shows the "Bachelor" and "Bachelorette," where the participants search for a spouse, are examples of our desire for companionship. This desire is displayed not only in media but in real life. People are searching for spouses, meaningful relationships, or friends. But whatever the search, there is only one true friendship that leads to greater relationships. As we strengthen our relationship with Christ, we can be assured that our secondary relationships will improve, as knowing Christ simply makes us all better.

REVEALING THE REAL YOU

But the Lord said to Samuel, "Do not look on his appearance or on the height of his stature, because I have rejected him. For the Lord sees not as man sees: man looks on the outward appearance, but the Lord looks on the heart."   1 Samuel 16:7 ESV

For we are his workmanship, created in Christ Jesus for good works, which God prepared beforehand, that we should walk in them.   Ephesians 2:10 ESV

I praise you, for I am fearfully and wonderfully made. Wonderful are your works; my soul knows it very well. My frame was not hidden from you, when I was being made in secret, intricately woven in the depths of the earth. Your eyes saw my unformed substance; in your book were written, every one of them, the days that were formed for me, when as yet there was none of them.

Psalm 139:14-16 ESV

Every so often, celebrities reveal themselves without makeup. For the most part, there is a drastic difference in their appearance. Few people would disagree about the impact Hollywood has on our appearances and our concepts of beauty. The irony of it all is that though celebrities account for such a small percentage of the population, their influence is remarkable. Despite their influence, many celebrities refuse to accept the responsibility of being a role model. They don't seem to care that their behavior—which is heavily scrutinized—is often emulated by the impressionable youth.

Given that many celebrities have handlers, spokespersons, publicists, a makeup team, bodyguards, and an entourage, their lifestyles are less normative. Many people are totally consumed by their fame. Whether we are talking about the fame and fortune of the Hollywood elite or the wealthiest Americans, many people who are outside of this reality are obsessed by this status. Perhaps the constant criticisms and scrutiny of celebrities is an attempt to normalize their bigger-than-life personas. However, it is unproductive to compare yourself to someone when it is likely that you will never meet them or ever understand the inherent complexities of their existence.

As we have seen in countless news reports, celebrities are not exempt from the difficulties of life but are under a great deal of pressure. These pressures include, but are not limited to, obsessions over their body image, massive insecurities, divorce, aging, financial responsibility, various legal matters, and the constant need to stay relevant. However, our fixation with celebrities distracts us from the most important task of dealing with our own issues. Thus, being consumed with a lifestyle that many celebrities admit is an illusion is not productive.

The Bible is clear that while the world places a high premium on our outward appearance, God looks inwardly at our heart. The heart should not consume itself with doing hair and makeup, presenting its chiseled physique, or boasting its financial status but should rely on the intangibles of life like love, kindness, happiness, and generosity to demonstrate its value. Celebrities, like every other individual, have to look in the mirror and face their truth. You cannot wear full makeup every single moment of your life, nor forever maintain the youthfulness of a twenty-year-old. While you can blanket your mattress with money, it cannot guarantee happiness. We must all face the realities of life, learn to accept our outward flaws, and be committed to ensuring our hearts are pure.

Today ask yourself, is your focus on outward appearance or on your heart? We are God's workmanship, and each of us is beautifully and wonderfully made to fulfill God's purpose for our lives. Even as a formless being, God saw your beauty and intricately made a masterpiece. Embrace your outward appearance, for it does not matter if you are big or small, rich or poor, tall or short, educated or not. To God, you are His greatest creation. When you truly know God, you simply have no problem revealing the real you.

A Deciding Life

Enter by the narrow gate. For the gate is wide and the way is easy that leads to destruction, and those who enter by it are many. For the gate is narrow and the way is hard that leads to life, and those who find it are few.   Matthew 7:13-14 ESV

There is a way that seems right to a man, but its end is the way to death.   Proverbs 14:12 ESV

In life, you quickly learn we all have to make choices irrespective of our starting points. Most neighborhoods are comprised of people who are affluent or those who are not financially stable but oftentimes their lives never interact. Although there are some neighborhoods where the entire community is wealthy, it is not normative as there are simply more people who are of a lower social status. Researchers in urban planning and sociologists have uncovered many of the inherent inequities in community development like food deserts, high concentrations of poverty, and redlining but despite these realities all people must make decisions. While the media attempts to force us to believe we are starkly different we certainly have more commonalities than others normally suggest. God instructs us all to make decisions, and He is not a respecter of persons. Money does not exempt you from His judgment, nor does poverty give you a pass for making poor decisions. Unfortunately, our justice system is not as fair and impartial as God's.

Due to the sad fact that it is tough on the streets of many neighborhoods across America, many kids feel that they have no choice but to make decisions that negatively impact their life chances. With futures built upon poor decisions and limited opportunity, they inevitably find themselves in the hands of a justice system that is embedded with inequalities. The same justice system that from time to time makes those who have power, money, and fame experience the consequences of their poor choices, often renders harsher judgments to minorities, treating them as though they grew up dreaming of being criminals, drug users, or failures. But these minorities faced realities that made them decide that a pathway to prison was more feasible than a college career at Princeton.

The Bible is clear that the narrow gate leading to salvation has few who enter, but the wide gate that leads to destruction has many. It only takes a fraction of a second to make a poor decision, but the consequences can span a lifetime. Therefore, it is imperative not to follow the path of man, but to follow the path of God.

Today is a day where you will make multiple decisions. Be sure those decisions are not informed by bitterness, blame, anger, or desperation. For the rich person who frequents the country club, do not drink and drive with confidence that your attorney can have the DUI charges dropped. For the poor person who cannot feed their family, do not steal from the local grocer with hopes that the judge will have leniency. It does not matter which side of the tracks you are from. Each day you must make choices, for we all have a deciding life.

Ageless Miracle

Then one of them said, "I will surely return to you about this time next year, and Sarah your wife will have a son." Now Sarah was listening at the entrance to the tent, which was behind him. Abraham and Sarah were already very old, and Sarah was past the age of childbearing. So Sarah laughed to herself as she thought, "After I am worn out and my lord is old, will I now have this pleasure?"

Genesis 18:10-12

So we do not lose heart. Though our outer self is wasting away, our inner self is being renewed day by day.   2 Corinthians 4:16 ESV

In today's society, we place a premium on youth and equate it with beauty and strength. However, the aging process does not deter God from blessing His children abundantly. Sarah was far past her childbearing years and when God promised her she would bear a child, all she could do was laugh. How many times have you heard others say the phrase, "I am too old?" It is imperative that you do not limit yourself because you are getting older. If you desire to return to school, start a business or even get married, it most certainly can be accomplished.

We are all in different stages of our lives, and we must learn to find joy in the aging process. For those who are younger, this message is important because when you are younger you desire to be older and gain independence. But soon you too will grow older. Do not rush it. For those who are already older, there is no point in living your life in the rear view mirror. The most important time of your life is what lies ahead, as God will renew your strength.

In an attempt to adjust to the aging process, we have adopted phrases like "fifty is the new thirty." Although people are living longer, fifty is still fifty. You must accept each phase of your life as a blessing. When you know God, you can look back over your entire life and proclaim the goodness of God, for you know you are an ageless miracle.

A DETERMINING FACTOR OF SUCCESS: EFFORT

The soul of the sluggard craves and gets nothing, while the soul of the diligent is richly supplied.   Proverbs 13:4 ESV

Whatever you do, work heartily, as for the Lord and not for men, knowing that from the Lord you will receive the inheritance as your reward. You are serving the Lord Christ.

Colossians 3:23-24 ESV

For even when we were with you, we would give you this command: If anyone is not willing to work, let him not eat.

2 Thessalonians 3:10 ESV

A slack hand causes poverty, but the hand of the diligent makes rich.   Proverbs 10:4 ESV

Some people are inclined to make excuses for their mediocrity and take absolutely no accountability for their station in life. Perhaps they were born into poverty, came from a dysfunctional home, lost a loved one, or had an abundance of unfortunate circumstances. However, these realities are often made worse by the poor decisions that accompany these situations.

When you talk with successful people about their rise to success, the conversation differs. Some people were born into families of wealth and others had to climb the ladder to gain upward mobility. But the common thread amongst those whose success is exemplary is hard work.

We live in a world where we tout the ideology of meritocracy, where talent and achievement are the primary indicators of success. But history has shown this is not always the case, as race and class can impede success for certain groups. For example, standardized tests were created to level the playing field for those who did not come from affluence and could not rely on the merits of their last name. In a perfect world, the standardized test would be exempt from cultural bias and serve as an accurate assessment of academic ability. But research has proven this is not the case. The reality is that the ascription of being born poor or from a certain ethnic group can impede success. But that is absolutely no excuse for laziness.

There are working-class families who are well below the poverty line and who reside in poor rural communities, yet they manage to work hard and send their children to college. Conversely, there are families in the same community who will work just as hard and not receive the same opportunities, but instead of complaining, they continue to work diligently.

Success, like many things, is relative. For example, some families believe raising their children to be responsible is an accomplishment while others might believe creating generational wealth and obtaining a prestigious career is the pinnacle of success. We can spend countless hours discussing divisive realities or we can agree that all people deserve a fair chance irrespective of race, class, gender, sexual orientation, ability, or religion.

In addition to understanding the need for equality, we must eliminate laziness for it accomplishes nothing and complains about everything. The Bible is clear that those who are lazy crave for nothing, but those who work hard have a burning desire to reach their potential. God rewards hard work even when society does not.

Today will you rise early or sleep in late? Will you apply to more jobs or will you put your job search on hold? Will you return to school or continue to complain about your low wages? Will you have a winning personality or a losing mentality? Will you continue to do what you have always done to get by or will you step outside of your comfort zone? Will you believe that God will reward your diligence or will you continue with your sluggish ways? The Bible says if you are not willing to work, you will not eat. This applies not only to physical food, but to spiritual food as well. We need God to feed our soul. Do not desire to be physically full but spiritually empty. A true determining factor of your success will always be the effort that you demonstrate.

BLINDED BY LIFE

As Jesus approached Jericho, a blind man was sitting by the roadside begging. When he heard the crowd going by, he asked what was happening. They told him, "Jesus of Nazareth is passing by."

He called out, "Jesus, Son of David, have mercy on me!" Those who led the way rebuked him and told him to be quiet, but he shouted all the more, "Son of David, have mercy on me!" Jesus stopped and ordered the man to be brought to him. When he came near, Jesus asked him, "What do you want me to do for you?" "Lord, I want to see," he replied. Jesus said to him, "Receive your sight; your faith has healed you." Immediately he received his sight and followed Jesus, praising God. When all the people saw it, they also praised God.   Luke 18:35-43

As Christians, you quickly understand life can knock the wind out of you without notice. For example, a forty-year-old woman who maintains a healthy lifestyle is diagnosed with terminal cancer. A rising athlete is gunned down on the city streets. Or perhaps a thirty-five-year-old man on his way home to his wife and three children is killed in a car accident. These are not fictitious accounts solely intended to grip one's emotions, but they serve as the unfortunate realities of life.

Living a good life or having an abundance of potential does not negate the fact that life happens. We can spend our time being depressed, angry, suicidal, blameworthy, emotionless, or bitter, but none of these reactions impede the current reality. Recently a woman who had experienced a peculiar cough visited the doctor and discovered she had lymph node cancer. She was immediately given intense treatment, but the cancer was spreading at a rapid rate and doctors could not contain it. However, countless loved ones and strangers prayed. Now the cancer is nonexistent. While this example has a great ending, the reality is that despite our brilliance, fortune, or prestige, we will all die one day.

But this reality should never weaken our trust in the Lord.

The blind beggar in the scripture relied on his sense of hearing and feeling. He felt the presence of the Lord and exclaimed, "Son of David, have mercy on me!" His sight was returned. Jesus stated, "Your faith has healed you." Some will read this and perhaps have some sadness because they prayed, cried, fasted, and hoped for a miracle, but their loved one succumbed to their illness. Maybe the dream you worked so tirelessly to fulfill never happened. The acceptance letter from college, the offer from an employer, or the approval for the home has yet to come. But if we would only hold on and wait for God's window of opportunity to open, we would experience His mercy.

Today even if the diagnosis is terminal, your faith must be unwavering. Some will be able to exclaim, "God has healed my body." Others will have to say, "My battle on earth has ended." God is awesome in life and death, tragedy and triumph, affluence and poverty, sickness and health. But we must understand that even when we are blinded by life, God will always return our sight. Can you see now?

LIVING LIFE WITHOUT REGRETS

> For godly grief produces a repentance that leads to salvation without regret, whereas worldly grief produces death.
>
> 2 Corinthians 7:10 ESV

Brothers, I do not consider that I have made it my own. But one thing I do: forgetting what lies behind and straining forward to what lies ahead, I press on toward the goal for the prize of the upward call of God in Christ Jesus. Let those of us who are mature think this way, and if in anything you think otherwise, God will reveal that also to you.   Philippians 3:13-15 ESV

There will be many moments of sadness and disappointments throughout your lifetime. As you cope with the realities of humanity, you quickly learn that regret can cause the greatest level of disappointment, as it restricts your ability to move forward. Even Jesus had to grapple with the difficulties of life. He experienced a wide range of emotions during the time of the crucifixion and was forced to make a decision whether or not to live with the regrets of disobedience and dishonor. The crucifixion and resurrection of Jesus Christ was the greatest demonstration of love without regrets as God sacrificed His Son for the sins of the world. He expressed His profound sense of abandonment as He was nailed to the cross saying, "My God, my God, why have you forsaken me?" (Mark 15:34). But that was almost immediately replaced with obedient submission as He uttered the words of Luke 23:46, "Father into your hands I commit my spirit."

How many times have you felt abandoned by God, as if He is not listening to your prayers of healing, reconciliation, prosperity, forgiveness, or protection? As Jesus struggled with his desire to live in the world, He felt forsaken. But as He reflected on God and His Kingdom, He was willing to submit himself as a sacrifice for our sins.

As it is written, regret in the world causes death. But if we repent for our sins we can truly live life without regrets. It is imperative that we press forward and forget what lies behind because failure to do so can create deep levels of regret. Today you must refuse to have regrets, as they will continue to impede your ability to achieve your destiny. If you want to return to school, if you want to forgive, if you want to love, if you want to be spontaneous, if you want to start a new career, if you want to travel, if you want to have a successful marriage, or if you want to be great then you must challenge yourself to move from wanting to doing. Desire + Inaction = Regret.

Time makes no apologies for its constant movement, and despite our rebellion it will move with or without us. Sadness can be overcome by happiness, sickness overcome by healing, pain overcome by forgiveness, death overcome by love, and regret overcome by doing. Thus, it is imperative we learn to live life without regrets.

GROWTH POTENTIAL

And so, from the day we heard, we have not ceased to pray for you, asking that you may be filled with the knowledge of his will in all spiritual wisdom and understanding, so as to walk in a manner worthy of the Lord, fully pleasing to him, bearing fruit in every good work and increasing in the knowledge of God.

Colossians 1:9-10 ESV

So put away all malice and all deceit and hypocrisy and envy and all slander. Like newborn infants, long for the pure spiritual milk, that by it you may grow up into salvation—if indeed you have tasted that the Lord is good. As you come to him, a living stone rejected by men but in the sight of God chosen and precious, you yourselves like living stones are being built up as a spiritual house, to be a holy priesthood, to offer spiritual sacrifices acceptable to God through Jesus Christ.   1 Peter 2:1-5 ESV

There is a huge difference between ignorance and stupidity, but oftentimes the words are used interchangeably. Ignorance is a lack of knowledge or information, whereas stupidity is based on one's lack of good sense or judgment. A one-year-old is ignorant about the potential safety hazard of not wearing a seat belt, whereas an adult who drives under the influence of alcohol is behaving stupidly, as their lack of judgment is endangering the lives of others and themselves.

In all of our relationships, we must discern if our behavior hinges on ignorance or stupidity, as either could affect growth potential. In the business world, if a company acquires another entity through acquisition or merger, it is imperative that the growth and stability are constantly scrutinized. Before companies like Facebook or Google even contemplate acquiring another company, they heavily monitor the company's financial health and their potential for growth.

Comparing the business function to the human function is by no means suggesting businesses always get it right. But their process of using analytics is one to be emulated. Imagine if we analyzed our relationships with the same analytical prowess that Fortune 500 companies apply when they are considering acquiring another company. Many women have blamed men for their failed relationships, saying that it is because they came from fatherless households. Similarly, men have been notorious for blaming women for their poor behavior, claiming that the women push them to this behavior by refusing to be submissive or by being incapable of listening. However, blaming the other person for your behavior is a classic case of not accepting responsibility. If in your lifetime you have had five relationships, which all ended badly, are you likely to say it is the fault of the five people or will you take a more individualized approach and analyze the one commonality within the scenario, which is yourself?

The Bible is clear that as we grow in our relationship with God, all of our relationships will become stronger if we apply our knowledge to combat ignorance and apply our wisdom to combat stupidity. God will fill you up. But if you are not careful, you will allow an undeserving person to deplete all of your resources. Today you can continue to blame your parents, your spouse, your significant other, or your friends for your mistakes. But did you ever analyze your relationships for growth? Ignorance keeps you in a continual uninformed state; stupidity causes you to willingly stay in a bad and unproductive situation. If your relationship is not growing, then you are operating with an extreme deficiency. If your newborn was not growing at a normal pace, you would quickly seek knowledge from the medical field to gain a better understanding about their condition. You would refuse to allow ignorance or stupidity to impede your child's development.

Perhaps you need to seek knowledge from God and analyze your personal relationships. An elevator that does not rise has absolutely no purpose. It is nothing more than a small room with a door. How long will you stand with someone who has no ability or interest to elevate your life? Take the time to analyze your relationships and discover if there is any growth potential.

THE ABILITY TO SERVE

You, my brothers and sisters, were called to be free. But do not use your freedom to indulge the flesh; rather, serve one another humbly in love. Galatians 5:13

God is not unjust; he will not forget your work and the love you have shown him as you have helped his people and continue to help them. Hebrews 6:10

Each of you should use whatever gift you have received to serve others, as faithful stewards of God's grace in its various forms.

1 Peter 4:10

As a child, you innately understand the words "me," "my," and "mine." As you become older, you quickly understand that such an open display of selfishness is not socially acceptable. However, as adults we are less likely to have temper tantrums because our friends are playing with our favorite toys. Unfortunately, some of us continue to struggle with sharing and serving others.

Jesus Christ is said to have lived for thirty-three years. But his short life was one of sacrifice, as He knew it was pleasing to God. He traveled from town to town feeding the hungry, healing the sick, raising the dead, and teaching the masses about the love of God. Despite His immeasurable sacrifice of time, talent, and resources, He would later be betrayed, denied, and crucified by the same people He helped. For the pessimist, this story is exactly what they envisioned. For the realist, this story exemplifies the human condition of selfishness. For the optimist, it is aligned with God's demand for service.

As a true servant of God, you must serve without expectations, understanding that it pleases God. Look to God, not humanity, to reward your service and commitment to others, for people can be selfish, unappreciative, and unmoved by your acts of service. Dr. Martin Luther King Jr. lived only thirty-nine years. At his funeral, in a prerecorded message he stated, "I'd like somebody to mention that day that Martin Luther King Jr. tried to give his life serving others. I'd like for somebody to say Martin Luther King Jr. tried to love somebody." On April 4, 1968, Dr. King was killed by an assassin's bullet but what is even more gripping is that he was there serving sanitation workers' demands for job safety, better wages and benefits, and union recognition. Although his previous visit to Memphis was plagued with violence, and his close associates attempted to convince him to abandon the mission, he returned to Memphis to serve others. This demonstration of service and commitment to others echoes his own words and is aligned with how God desires us to be servants.

To be a servant does not appear to be a glamorous and rewarding job but it unequivocally demonstrates our love for God. Today is the perfect day for you to serve others without expectations. Perhaps you can work in a food pantry, open a door, give up your seat on a crowded train, encourage someone, purchase clothes for a needy family, listen to someone, or volunteer at a homeless shelter or hospital. But whatever you decide to do, do it for the right reasons. True servants are not looking for a reward or an abundance of recognition but are serving others as a means to serve the Lord. God has gifted each of us with talents and resources. If we fail to serve others, we are essentially telling God we are not grateful. We must not revert to an ideology of me, my, and mine as it relates to our talents and resources, but must be openly willing to share and serve. Even in death, the compassion and love of a servant will always remain. Thus, there is simply nothing greater than the ability to serve.

THE ENEMY SPEAKS YOUR LANGUAGE: WISDOM OVERCOMES TEMPTATION

Now the serpent was more crafty than any of the wild animals the Lord God had made. He said to the woman, "Did God really say, 'You must not eat from any tree in the garden'?" The woman said to the serpent, "We may eat fruit from the trees in the garden, but God did say, 'You must not eat fruit from the tree that is in the middle of the garden, and you must not touch it, or you will die.'" "You will not certainly die," the serpent said to the woman. "For God knows that when you eat from it your eyes will be opened, and you will be like God, knowing good and evil." When the woman saw that the fruit of the tree was good for food and pleasing to the eye, and also desirable for gaining wisdom, she took some and ate it. She also gave some to her husband, who was with her, and he ate it.   Genesis 3:1-6

Then Jesus was led by the Spirit into the wilderness to be tempted by the devil. After fasting forty days and forty nights, he was hungry. The tempter came to him and said, "If you are the Son of God, tell these stones to become bread." Jesus answered, "It is written: 'Man shall not live on bread alone, but on every word that comes from the mouth of God.'" Then the devil took him to the holy city and had him stand on the highest point of the temple. "If you are the Son of God," he said, "throw yourself down. For it is written: 'He will command his angels concerning you, and they will lift you up in their hands, so that you will not strike your foot against a stone.'" Jesus answered him, "It is also written: 'Do not put the Lord your God to the test.'" Again, the devil took him to a very high mountain and showed him all the kingdoms of the world and their splendor. "All this I will give you," he said, "if you will bow down and worship me." Jesus said to him, "Away from me, Satan! For it is written: 'Worship the Lord your God, and serve him only.'" Then the devil left him, and angels came and attended him. Matthew 4:1-11

In the story of creation, we learn about the weaknesses of humanity and our desire to have more than what God has provided. Adam and Eve were given all of the Garden of Eden, with only one limitation: do not eat from the Forbidden Tree, as it would bring destruction to the world. On the other hand, Jesus was tempted in the wilderness and Satan tried to use biblical truths to manipulate Jesus into forfeiting His beliefs. The difference between Adam and Eve and Jesus is that Jesus used wisdom to overcome the schemes and deception of the enemy, whereas Adam and Eve succumbed to their selfish desires. Satan's mode of attack is not highly intelligent. He simply exploits people's weaknesses and uses crafty methods to make others try to deter you from your destiny.

Many people misinterpret this common scripture and suggest Eve caused the fall of humanity. Although Eve was the first to eat from the Forbidden Tree, Adam could have denied her offer, as he was directly instructed by God not to eat from the tree. Unfortunately, many of us are similar to Adam and Eve. We know what we should not do and are aware of the consequences, but we foolishly do as we desire.

Imagine after being in the desert for forty days and forty nights how hungry and exhausted Jesus must have been. Satan's modus operandi is to attack us in our weakest moment, in hopes that we will concede to our exhaustion. However, Jesus was not willing to be manipulated by Satan and did not turn stones into bread, fall from the highest point of the temple, nor worship Satan in exchange for all the kingdoms of the world. Instead, He boldly said, "Away from me Satan!" Today who will you be like, Adam and Eve or Jesus?

We are faced with choices every single day, and we must be cognizant of how those choices greatly affect our lives, whether in a good way or a bad way. Are you someone who wants more than God has provided? Are you someone who is easily tricked by the craftiness of Satan? Are you someone who is willing to gamble with your gifts, talents, and purpose in exchange for an empty promise? Or are you someone who is not moved by the enemy's trickery, deception, and manipulation? If you want to defend yourself from the persuasive tactics of the enemy, you must be aware of a couple of things: one, the enemy speaks your language; and two, you must possess wisdom to overcome temptation.

fear not, for I am with you;   be not dismayed, for I am your God; I will strengthen you, I will help you, I will uphold you with my righteous right hand.

Isaiah 41:10 ESV

REFLECTION 6

GREED: A SILENT KILLER

You ask and do not receive, because you ask wrongly, to spend it on your passions.   James 4:3 ESV

A greedy man stirs up strife, but the one who trusts in the Lord will be enriched.   Proverbs 28:25 ESV

But those who desire to be rich fall into temptation, into a snare, into many senseless and harmful desires that plunge people into ruin and destruction.   1 Timothy 6:9 ESV

One gives freely, yet grows all the richer; another withholds what he should give, and only suffers want.   Proverbs 11:24 ESV

According to the Merriam-Webster Dictionary, greed is a selfish desire to have more of something (especially money). We live in a world that is motivated by money. Most people assume those who have an abundance of financial resources are exempt from many problems experienced by those of lower financial means. But this is untrue. No one is exempt from the wrath of God, for He is merciful, and He is also just but we must also be mindful of the consequences of poor decisions.

Not all poor people are the same. Likewise, not all rich people are the same. Some want to be rich so they can help others, but there are those who want to be rich for all the wrong reasons. Money will expose your true character. If you are a selfish person with little, you most certainly will be a selfish person with much.

While God does not condemn prosperity, the Bible is clear about the pitfalls of seeking wealth for selfish reasons. Those who obtain their financial success for selfish reasons will experience destruction. That destruction can come in the form of losing everything or having everything, but feeling as though you have nothing. If you gained your success from greed, your primary focus was to take from others in order to satisfy your own passions. Oftentimes, God will not allow this person's desires to materialize.

Those who have a strong desire to be rich must understand that temptation will meet them at their doorstep, offering an illusion of happiness and a thirst for power that no amount of ambition or talent can fulfill. We must learn to give freely, as it allows us to grow richer in our love for God. Restricting our resources for the sake of greed will only bring discontentment. Today is the perfect day to rid yourself of selfish desires and to discontinue your race toward wealth, given that it's predicated on greed. The Bible says that a greedy person stirs up strife, but the person who trusts God more than their bank accounts will be eternally rich. The power of God allows the impoverished person to receive grace and spiritual richness, despite their perceived economic state. However, those who can buy whatever earthly possessions they desire will never be able to purchase salvation.

In a perfect world, even if everyone did not have enough, they still would be willing to share. But the sad reality is that capitalism, consumerism, and meritocracy all undergird greed. Capitalism is based on competition and wealth accumulation. Consumerism believes it is good to spend an abundance of money on goods and services. Meritocracy believes that hard work is the greatest determinant of achievement.

However, everything in the world belongs to God. He does not need a free market to produce competition, an outrageous price tag to indicate worth, or the merits of hard work to produce success. He is God all by Himself. Therefore, it is imperative that you understand that greed is a silent killer aimed to rob you of your eternity.

THE HEALING HANDS OF JESUS

Fear not, for I am with you; be not dismayed, for I am your God; I will strengthen you, I will help you, I will uphold you with my righteous right hand.   Isaiah 41:10 ESV

Heal me, O Lord, and I shall be healed; save me, and I shall be saved, for you are my praise.   Jeremiah 17:14 ESV

But he was pierced for our transgressions; he was crushed for our iniquities; upon him was the chastisement that brought us peace, and with his wounds we are healed.   Isaiah 53:5 ESV

Behold, I will bring to it health and healing, and I will heal them and reveal to them abundance of prosperity and security.

Jeremiah 33:6 ESV

Bless the Lord, O my soul, and forget not all his benefits, who forgives all your iniquity, who heals all your diseases, who redeems your life from the pit, who crowns you with steadfast love and mercy, who satisfies you with good so that your youth is renewed like the eagle's. Psalm 103:2-5 ESV

Each day a patient hears disheartening news from a doctor, whether it is that they will have to be prepped for immediate surgery to repair a blocked artery or that they are diagnosed with a terminal disease. Although the patient is understandably devastated, God is not moved. Anthony Yahle, a thirty-seven-year-old man from Ohio, was declared dead after a forty-five-minute attempt to resuscitate him. But his seventeen-year-old son yelled into his room, "Dad, you're not going to die today." Shortly after the son's defiant yell for God's mercy, the man had a faint heartbeat and fully recovered without any additional treatment. He soon returned home to his family. Doctors have yet to provide an explanation for his medical outcome.

Even more shocking was an eighty-seven-year-old man from Mississippi named Walter Williams who had been pronounced dead by the coroner and placed in a body bag when the mortician noticed his leg moving. That man is now alive. The news reporters jokingly claimed that perhaps the coroner made a mistake. But the family was convinced that it was a gift from God.

In life, you will always have those who discredit the miraculous power of God and give doctors praise without ever acknowledging God. Even when a person is surrounded by family and friends while they combat disease and undergo surgery and recovery, it is imperative that they maintain supernatural strength. When you hear bad news from doctors, it creates a number of emotions, ranging from sadness to defiance. You begin to question God and ask why. You begin to think about your mortality. You think about your relationship with Christ. You think about your loved ones. You reflect on those who have endured similar circumstances. But your greatest focus should be on the power of God, for only He has the power to restore your health.

Today I declare that God will strengthen you. I declare that God will redeem you from your fear. And I declare that by His stripes you are healed. You will return to the strength of your youth and soar like an eagle, for you now know the healing hands of Jesus.

HAPPY FOR THE RIGHT REASONS

I perceived that there is nothing better for them than to be joyful and to do good as long as they live; 13 also that everyone should eat and drink and take pleasure in all his toil—this is God's gift to man.   Ecclesiastes 3:12-13 ESV

Let not your hearts be troubled. Believe in God; believe also in me.   John 14:1 ESV

Oh, taste and see that the Lord is good! Blessed is the man who takes refuge in him!   Psalm 34:8 ESV

We spend a great deal of time chasing temporal happiness. Oftentimes we forget that success, material wealth, health, and life circumstances are subject to change at any moment. What happens when the wealthy person makes a wrong financial decision and loses everything, or the vegan and fitness guru becomes terminally ill? If you live long enough, you will quickly learn that time is a fleeting reality. Knowing this makes maximizing each second imperative.

Singer, producer, and songwriter Pharrell Williams has a smash hit single titled "Happy" that has gone viral on the Internet and has topped the charts globally. The premise of the song is simple: it boldly celebrates happiness. However, a deeper understanding of happiness is needed, as the Bible is clear that joy is God's gift to humanity. It is written that our lives are promised pain, but if we trust in the Lord at all times, He can sooth our troubled hearts. We must take refuge in the Lord.

Today, I am happy whether I am healthy or sick, rich or poor, employed or unemployed, young or old, single or married, in the valley or on the mountaintop. That is because happiness is not contingent on superficial things but is truly a gift from God. Are you happy for the right reasons?

BOLD UNDER PRESSURE

Consider it a sheer gift, friends, when tests and challenges come at you from all sides. You know that under pressure, your faith-life is forced into the open and shows its true colors. So don't try to get out of anything prematurely. Let it do its work so you become mature and well developed, not deficient in any way. If you don't know what you're doing, pray to the Father. He loves to help. You'll get his help, and won't be condescended to when you ask for it. Ask boldly, believingly, without a second thought. People who "worry their prayers" are like wind-whipped waves. Don't think you're going to get anything from the Master that way, adrift at sea, keeping all your options open. When down-and-outers get a break, cheer! And when the arrogant rich are brought down to size, cheer! Prosperity is as short-lived as a wildflower, so don't ever count on it. You know that as soon as the sun rises, pouring down its scorching heat, the flower withers. Its petals wilt and, before you know it, that beautiful face is a barren stem. Well, that's a picture of the "prosperous life." At the very moment everyone is looking on in admiration, it fades away to nothing. Anyone who meets a testing challenge head-on and manages to stick it out is mighty fortunate. For such persons loyally in love with God, the reward is life and more life. Don't let anyone under pressure to give in to evil say, "God is trying to trip me up." God is impervious to evil, and puts evil in no one's way.

James 1:2-13 MSG

Everyone handles pressure differently. But for Christians, pressure should become our platform to display our faith in the Lord. It is easy to praise God when everything is seemingly going great, but what happens when the pressures of life become overbearing? It is our inclination to instantly release pressure. However, God does not desire for us to escape prematurely, and often He restricts our options to ensure that we get the inherent lesson. The pressure allows us to mature in our faith so that we can become bolder in our declarations for God.

Perhaps you are working for an employer that does not recognize your talents. Or maybe you are living in a home that no longer serves your needs. You could be in a relationship that has grown stale, or in your last semester of school and the pressure of it all weighs heavy on your spirit. But you must hold on. Learn to pray boldly to the Father, knowing that He will provide the answers you desire.

Life has swift transitions. The rich can instantly become poor, the healthy can become sick, the novice can become the expert, and the underdog can become the champion. Today you must face the pressure head on, as you know this is only a test of your faith. Do not allow the pressure to cause you to give in to evil and doubt, but trust in the Lord at all times.

If you lose your fortune, will you trust Him? If you become homeless, will you trust Him? If your health fails, will you trust Him? If your marriage ends in divorce, will you trust Him? If you lose your job, will you trust Him? If it seems as if He is not listening, will you trust Him? The Bible says that God does not put evil in anyone's way. Therefore, do not fold under pressure. Instead, be bold under pressure.

Living a Life of Expectancy

For I know the plans I have for you, declares the Lord, plans for welfare and not for evil, to give you a future and a hope.

Jeremiah 29:11 ESV

Sometimes you can feel as if you have no clue what the future entails or why life is so difficult. But God has no worries, for He knows your destiny. The Bible says that in this life we are promised pain, and it is that pain or trouble which causes us to have reservations about our future. You can no longer allow the past to dictate your future because despite your mistakes, God still has plans for your life.

We have a tendency to create our own elaborate plans based on shallow endeavors, and typically these plans falter. Sometimes it is because we are not focused on ourselves, but on the talents of others. If you desire to be an entertainer because you are mesmerized by fame and fortune but lack talent, then chances are you will not be successful. If you want to become a doctor because your parents are doctors but lack passion for the practice, then chances are you will not be successful. If you want to become an attorney because you have a passion for justice and a desire for the courtroom but lack the talent of research, then chances are you will not be successful. These assertions are not always true. But what they suggest is that in order for plans for the future to materialize, your desire has to be more than a superficial notion. In fact, your plans must be in line with the will of God. Otherwise, your plans are merely foolish ambition.

Today you must decide to embrace a future that is free from get-rich-quick schemes, competition fueled by jealousy or dreams based on popular culture. God has endorsed your future. In fact, God knows the plans He has for you. He sees your future as one with hope and not evil. Therefore, you must live your life with expectancy and unequivocally know that your future will be great.

The Last Days of Christ: Betrayal, Denial, Crucifixion, Death, and Resurrection

"Rise! Let us go! Here comes my betrayer!" While he was still speaking, Judas, one of the Twelve, arrived. With him was a large crowd armed with swords and clubs, sent from the chief priests and the elders of the people. Now the betrayer had arranged a signal with them: "The one I kiss is the man; arrest him."

Matthew 26:46-48

Then he began to call down curses, and he swore to them, "I don't know the man!" Immediately a rooster crowed. Then Peter remembered the word Jesus had spoken: "Before the rooster crows, you will disown me three times." And he went outside and wept bitterly.

Matthew 26:74-75

They stripped him and put a scarlet robe on him, and then twisted together a crown of thorns and set it on his head. They put a staff in his right hand. Then they knelt in front of him and mocked him. "Hail, king of the Jews!" they said. They spit on him, and took the staff and struck him on the head again and again. After they had mocked him, they took off the robe and put his own clothes on him. Then they led him away to crucify him.   Matthew 27:28-31

And when Jesus had cried out again in a loud voice, he gave up his spirit. At that moment the curtain of the temple was torn in two from top to bottom. The earth shook, the rocks split and the tombs broke open. The bodies of many holy people who had died were raised to life.   Matthew 27:50-51

The angel said to the women, Do not be afraid, for I know that you are looking for Jesus, who was crucified. He is not here; he has risen, just as he said. Come and see the place where he lay.
                                            Matthew 28: 5-6

Perhaps you are having an eventful week. Maybe your job is causing stress, your family affairs are in shambles, or your health is declining. But all of these events combined cannot reflect the torment that Jesus was subjected to.

The story of Jesus is dynamic, for it is not just filled with miracles, compassion, and love, it shows the vileness of humanity. Although the death of Jesus happened more than two thousand years ago, there are many lessons within the captivating narrative.

Lesson one: just because you love your enemies and provide for them, does not mean that they will not betray you. However, God will promote you while destroying their endeavors. Judas, the betrayer, committed suicide because the thirty silver coins he received for betraying Jesus could not bandage his guilt and shame. Lesson two: loyalty in words means nothing when you fail to have loyalty in action. Peter, the aggressive and vocal servant of Jesus, denied the Lord, even though he claimed to love Him more than anyone else loved Him. Lesson three: the purpose is always greater than the pain. While theologians, historians, and movie producers have attempted to depict the brutality of the crucifixion, the greater focus should always be on the purpose. Jesus was sent to save humanity, not Himself. Lesson four: death is only final if you make it, but love is immortal. Lesson five: wait for God to remove the stone.

Believers all around the world celebrate the resurrection of Christ. But above Jesus rising, the more compelling reality is His willingness to die so that we could have the right relationship with God. What are you willing to let go of in an effort to be closer to God? Let go of jealousy, bitterness, brokenness, blame, guilt, pain, hurt, shame, fear, insecurity, or anything that impedes your relationship with Christ. Though my friends betray me, deny they know me, beg for my public suffering, attempt to kill me, still I rise.

CHOOSE YOUR TEAM WISELY

One of those days, Jesus went out to a mountainside to pray, and spent the night praying to God. When morning came, he called his disciples to him and chose twelve of them, whom he also designated apostles: Simon (whom he named Peter), his brother Andrew, James, John, Philip, Bartholomew, Matthew, Thomas, James son of Alphaeus, Simon who was called the Zealot, Judas son of James, and Judas Iscariot, who became a traitor.   Luke 6:12-16

In modern society, corporations have a large expenditure for recruiting. For more prestigious employment opportunities like selecting a Chief Executive Officer; they undergo a meticulous process, as they understand that making an error in judgment can be dire to the overall stability of the company. Jesus of Nazareth had the daunting task of selecting twelve disciples who would be commissioned to serve as messengers of the good news. However, prior to making His decision, he prayed to His Father, as such decisions should not be made without God's approval.

It is interesting to learn how those He selected responded to His call.

> As Jesus was walking beside the Sea of Galilee, he saw two brothers, Simon called Peter and his brother Andrew. They were casting a net into the lake, for they were fishermen. "Come, follow me," Jesus said, "and I will send you out to fish for people." At once they left their nets and followed him. Going on from there, he saw two other brothers, James son of Zebedee and his brother John. They were in a boat with their father Zebedee, preparing their nets. Jesus called them, and immediately they left the boat and their father and followed him.   Matthew 4:18-22

In a real sense, what are you willing to leave behind in order to live the life that God intended? Some people refuse to accept certain positions that have great promise because it would require them to leave their hometown. As it seems, some of God's greatest plans require you to step outside of your comfort zone and even outside of logic. For example, you are a vice president of a major corporation but despite the demands of your job, you have always remained a faithful servant.

God reveals to you in a dream to move your family to an indigenous country for two years to do missionary work. What makes the decision even more challenging is that you have been asked to accept the position of Chief Operating Officer for the Southwest Region. Both offers require relocating your family. Where do you go? This decision is one that the twelve apostles had to grapple with, but without hesitation, they followed Jesus and left everything behind.

Today you must ask yourself what your partnerships, friendships, and relationships indicate about your success. Jesus knew that Judas Iscariot would betray Him. However, prior to the betrayal, it is not written that Judas had a disdain for Jesus or harbored jealousy, but that he was selected by God to fulfill the promise. But do not interpret this to mean that God invites you to allow envious people to be in your circle just because they might eventually serve a good purpose. True friends or partners are not in competition with you, but fully understand their role and believe the relationship is far greater than any individual gain.

After the resurrection and ascension, the apostles went out to spread the word of God. Many of them were martyred for their beliefs. In the end, Jesus had formed partnerships that were indestructible. Therefore, if you want success, you must choose your team wisely.

WE ARE FAMILY

Thus there were fourteen generations in all from Abraham to David, fourteen from David to the exile to Babylon, and fourteen from the exile to the Messiah.   Matthew 1:17

It almost seems commonplace to talk about the inherent dysfunction within our families, irrespective of race or class. Given that there are no perfect people, it is safe to say there are no perfect families. However, some people believe their families have abandoned them, and their issues are too painful to forgive. These realities create unnecessary tension among families. As a result, some family members will spend years harboring resentment towards their loved ones.

The genealogy of Jesus lets us know that our families are more robust than our immediate family unit. Like Jesus, we are tied to many generations. A child does not ask to be born into this world nor can they select their family, which implies that our genealogy is from God. Many people have traced their family history and discovered the multiple generations of their lineage. It is imperative that we find contentment in the families God has placed us in, but with the understanding that our families will never be perfect.

Unfortunately, it takes a tragedy to put some families back together. But those families would be so much better had they resolved their issues sooner. Your grandparents, parents, children, siblings, aunts, uncles, nieces, nephews, cousins, and in-laws are all a part of your family. Each one is like a puzzle piece. They all serve an integral part in your life. Today resolve any issues of the past, enjoy the moments of the present, and hope for a brighter tomorrow, as this will forever be your family. Through the pain and through the joy, we are family.

A Mother's Story

This is how the birth of Jesus the Messiah came about: His mother Mary was pledged to be married to Joseph, but before they came together, she was found to be pregnant through the Holy Spirit. Because Joseph her husband was faithful to the law, and yet did not want to expose her to public disgrace, he had in mind to divorce her quietly.   Matthew 1:18-19

Near the cross of Jesus stood his mother, his mother's sister, Mary the wife of Clopas, and Mary Magdalene. When Jesus saw his mother there, and the disciple whom he loved standing nearby, he said to her, "Woman, here is your son," and to the disciple, "Here is your mother." From that time on, this disciple took her into his home.   John 19:25-27

Every child has a mother and father, as it is impossible to conceive without the mother's egg being fertilized by the father's sperm. In the Bible, Joseph understood this concept and could not understand how Mary became pregnant, as she was a virgin. But through a dream, it was revealed that she was impregnated by the Holy Spirit. The Bible does not give us the full trajectory of Jesus' life, but we are given extensive knowledge about his birth and death. In the scriptures, we see the endearing and enduring love that Mary had for her Son.

Mary fled to Egypt to protect her infant Son from King Herod, who had ordered that all children two years old and younger be killed. At the cross, it was Mary who witnessed her Son being murdered. As He looked into her eyes, He felt her unwavering love. As is the way of a loving mother, she was with Him from the beginning to the end.

Today whether you have a great relationship with your mother, or it needs to be repaired, do not lose sight of a mother's story, which is filled with love, protection, and strength. For those whose mothers have passed away, reflect on the memories she left behind. For those who were abandoned or mistreated, forgive your mother, as she made a great decision to birth you into the world.

A mother's story will not always be perfect or delightful, but it is sometimes filled with mistakes and regrets. Yet none of it negates the fact that she is your mother. She is a mother to be cherished, a mother to be forgiven, a mother to be honored, and a mother to be loved. It will never be perfect, but it will always be a mother's story.

You are Not Alone

Be strong and courageous. Do not fear or be in dread of them, for it is the LORD your God who goes with you. He will not leave you or forsake you. Then Moses summoned Joshua and said to him in the sight of all Israel, "Be strong and courageous, for you shall go with this people into the land that the LORD has sworn to their fathers to give them, and you shall put them in possession of it. It is the LORD who goes before you. He will be with you; he will not leave you or forsake you. Do not fear or be dismayed."

Deuteronomy 31:6-8 ESV

Keep your life free from love of money, and be content with what you have, for he has said, "I will never leave you nor forsake you."

Hebrews 13:5 ESV

Have I not commanded you? Be strong and courageous. Do not be frightened, and do not be dismayed, for the Lord your God is with you wherever you go.

Joshua 1:9 ESV

Most people claim to have friends and find pleasure in spending time with those whom they love. But there will come a time when only God can bring you comfort. We place great value on relationships, but even the greatest ones are riddled with disappointments. If we all had what we needed in each other, we would have no need for God.

Moses constantly prayed for strength and guidance to lead his people to the Promised Land, and God assured him that He would never leave or forsake him. Sometimes when life pushes us to the edge, we consequently try to find comfort in people and things. But they are incapable of fulfilling our desires. God instructs us to be free from the love of money, as we will begin to believe money has more power than God. Money cannot rid us of disease or natural disaster, but can only afford an illusion of happiness, safety, and power. It is imperative to find contentment in what you have and not worry about the things you lack, as God will provide.

Lastly, God instructs us to be strong and courageous. Despite the transitions of life, we need not be fearful or dismayed. As you sit in a room filled with people but feel isolated, know that you are not alone. If we would only rely on the power of God, we would realize that we are not alone. It is in times of need that we can evaluate the loyalty, dependability, trust, and love of our family and friends, which, unfortunately, are flawed. However, no matter how low you become or how isolated you feel, God promises to never leave or forsake you, which simply means you are not alone.

He holds success in store for the upright, he is a shield to those whose walk is blameless, for he guards the course of the just and protects the way of his faithful ones. *Proverbs 2:7–8*

REFLECTION 7

THE RIGHT TIME

For the revelation awaits an appointed time; it speaks of the end and will not prove false. Though it linger, wait for it; it will certainly come and will not delay.   Habakkuk 2:3

For we are God's handiwork, created in Christ Jesus to do good works, which God prepared in advance for us to do.
                                                    Ephesians 2:10

We do not want you to become lazy, but to imitate those who through faith and patience inherit what has been promised.
                                                    Hebrews 6:12

Even youths grow tired and weary, and young men stumble and fall; but those who hope in the Lord will renew their strength. They will soar on wings like eagles; they will run and not grow weary, they will walk and not be faint.   Isaiah 40: 30-31

Oftentimes we find ourselves becoming impatient, as our current circumstances seem too difficult to bear without the intercession of God.

But despite our panic, the wait continues. The Bible is clear that if we would maintain our faith, the will of God will not prove to be false. We must be cognizant of the father and child relationship dynamic that we have with Christ. We are no different from children asking their parents to buy them a new toy. The child will make promises in an effort to convince their parents that the purchasing of this new toy will help them listen better and do their chores without being asked. But the parents are wise enough to know that these are empty promises.

As a Christian, how many times have you attempted to bargain with God, hoping it would expedite your desires? For example, you have a desire to find another job, as you believe your current job has no growth potential. But after several months of trying, you are not successful. In your desperation, you uttered this phrase: God if you give me this job, I will cherish it and will not be stagnate, but will seek all the opportunities for advancement. However, God still made you wait, and it took you more than two years to find employment. Later you understood why God made you wait. You read in the newspaper or heard on a newscast that the majority of jobs you had applied for had experienced massive layoffs or suffered other internal issues that would have more than likely resulted in your termination.

God has called us to do good works, and He never sends us on assignment without fully equipping us with the tools we need. Perhaps God has you waiting because He knows you are not ready for what's to come. If you do not become lazy, weary, or impatient, He will provide the inheritance that He has already predestined you to receive.

Today despite your eagerness or desperation, it is imperative that you patiently wait on the Lord. If God says no or not now, do not try to bargain with Him, as your negotiation skills are insufficient. We live in a "right now" society and are led to believe that we must have all things instantaneously. But such a notion is outside of the teachings of the Bible. Did Sarah have to wait to birth a child? Did the children of Israel have to wait to receive the Promised Land? Did humanity have to wait for the Messiah? We all have to wait for something, but when we are waiting on God to fulfill a promise, we can be assured that He will deliver, and His timing is always the right time.

THE COST OF DISOBEDIENCE

Now the serpent was more crafty than any of the wild animals the Lord God had made. He said to the woman, "Did God really say, 'You must not eat from any tree in the garden'?" The woman said to the serpent, "We may eat fruit from the trees in the garden, but God did say, 'You must not eat fruit from the tree that is in the middle of the garden, and you must not touch it, or you will die.'" "You will not certainly die," the serpent said to the woman. "For God knows that when you eat from it your eyes will be opened, and you will be like God, knowing good and evil." When the woman saw that the fruit of the tree was good for food and pleasing to the eye, and also desirable for gaining wisdom, she took some and ate it. She also gave some to her husband, who was with her, and he ate it. Then the eyes of both of them were opened, and they realized they were naked; so they sewed fig leaves together and made coverings for themselves. Then the man and his wife heard the sound of the Lord God as he was walking in the garden in the cool of the day, and they hid from the Lord God among the trees of the garden. But the Lord God called to the man, "Where are you?" Genesis 3:1-9

The story of Adam and Eve is intriguing, as it represents the rigid dichotomy of the rise and fall of humanity. Of all of God's creations, He considered humanity to be His greatest. After all, we were made in His image and His likeness.

As it is written, Adam was given a helper called Eve. From his flesh, she was created. Both were instructed not to eat from the forbidden tree, but the serpent was crafty and misstated God's instructions in order to manipulate their desire for wisdom. It is when we are weak and vulnerable that the world will offer us the greatest level of temptation.

As a result of Adam and Eve's disobedience, there were grave consequences for everyone. The serpent was cursed to live on his belly and crawl while eating dirt. The woman would experience severe pain in childbirth. As for the man, the ground was cursed so that his days would be filled with painful toil. Disobedience is extremely displeasing to God.

If only Adam and Eve had found contentment in all that they had, our world would be free from evil. Unfortunately, humanity's inability to obey forced God to flood the earth, and all those outside of Noah's ark perished.

Each of us will have someone who represents a serpent aimed to destroy our destiny. Please understand that if you allow them to lead you into disobedience, God will come looking for you. Try as you may to hide, He knows exactly where you are. Your attempts at explaining and rationalizing will not impede His wrath. As there are simply no perfect people in the world, we will all disappoint God despite our greatest efforts to please Him. But because of the blood of Christ, we can seek forgiveness for our sins. However, we must not foolishly be disobedient, believing that God will grant us a pass for our actions, for though our sins might range from a small untruth to a heinous murder, there is a cost for disobedience. Are you willing to pay God's price?

SUCCESS IS FOUND IN THE DEEP: DIG FOR IT

Blessed is the one who does not walk in step with the wicked or stand in the way that sinners take or sit in the company of mockers, but whose delight is in the law of the Lord, and who meditates on his law day and night. That person is like a tree planted by streams of water, which yields its fruit in season and whose leaf does not wither—whatever they do prospers.   Psalm 1:1-3

Beware! Guard against every kind of greed. Life is not measured by how much you own.   Luke 12:15 NLT

Do not lay up for yourselves treasures on earth, where moth and rust destroy and where thieves break in and steal, but lay up for yourselves treasures in heaven, where neither moth nor rust destroys and where thieves do not break in and steal. For where your treasure is, there your heart will be also.   Matthew 6:19-21 ESV

From an early age, we are taught about success and failure. Young children are told of the importance of education, responsibility, and leadership, but we all are influenced by the powerful undertones of society, which indicate what it means to be successful. At your local grocer, you will find magazines that feature some of the top celebrities in Hollywood, and you can learn about their lives, ranging from their fashion to their dietary regimen. Billboards, television, and web search engines are constantly providing subliminal messages about the concept and image of success. Our notions of success have a strong element of greed.

Yet, the Bible does not indict financial success. Nor does it endorse extreme poverty as a means to please God. But it clearly states that success is more than your earthly possessions. Someone who is blessed by God stands outside of the purview of society's' standard. Believing they are more than a collection of worldly possessions and trivial accomplishments, they live their life like a tree firmly planted in God's word. This concept directly diminishes the storyline of societal success, even though we are inundated with lists of the most powerful and richest people in the world.

It is important to understand that today if you desire to acquire success, it is best you do it as God intended and become firmly planted in His word. To be firmly planted, you must be willing to explore the deep and dig for it, as success is not found on the surface.

A Father Protects

He holds success in store for the upright, he is a shield to those whose walk is blameless, for he guards the course of the just and protects the way of his faithful ones.   Proverbs 2:7-8

You are my hiding place; you will protect me from trouble and surround me with songs of deliverance.   Psalm 32:7

Do not withhold your mercy from me, Lord; may your love and faithfulness always protect me.   Psalm 40:11

Many children have a great relationship with their father and can vividly recall fond moments of their childhood. Perhaps you recall you and your dad working in the garage, him cheering at your games, the two of you playing in the backyard, him teaching you how to drive, or him meeting your significant other for the first time. These memories allow you to understand his compassion and love.

However, fathers are not without flaws. Some children's memories are clouded with wavering emotions, as their dad was hardly ever home due to an extensive work schedule. Or maybe he played a passive role in their lives, which strained the relationship. Then there are those children whose fathers represent grave disappointment, as they cowardly decided to abandon their children altogether and allow them to navigate this world seemingly alone.

Our earthly father is not without blemish. But our heavenly Father is blameless, and His primary role is to protect His children. If we are in trouble, He will serve as our hiding place. His love and mercy will protect us, and He will bring success to those who love Him by guarding the course of their lives.

The child who received love from their earthly father always remembers the joy it brought. Conversely, those who did not receive love never forget the emptiness their fathers' abandonment caused. But God will protect those who are seemingly alone. Oftentimes those children who are abandoned will become successful despite the unnecessary obstacles created by their absent father, as God will navigate their path.

When you truly understand the love of the Father and the love of the Son, it makes it easy for you to overflow the hearts of your children with love. Today what you must understand is that you are loved. Whether you have a great relationship with your earthly father or whether it is estranged, God loves you immensely. A coward abandons his children, but a father will die to protect them.

Hope In Waiting

I would have despaired unless I had believed that I would see the goodness of the Lord In the land of the living. Wait for the Lord; Be strong and let your heart take courage; Yes, wait for the Lord.

Psalm 27:13-14 NASB

No one who hopes in you will ever be put to shame, but shame will come on those who are treacherous without cause. Psalm 25:3

Although we may be discouraged during the waiting process. Our waiting is coupled with hope in the Lord, we do not despair but are encouraged that God will deliver us in the land of the living.

However, waiting can be extremely difficult. Try telling a person who has been faithfully searching for employment without success that their waiting is necessary. Question parents who have been waiting for five years to receive an organ transplant for their child. Or ask a woman who desires to give birth but continues to have complications if waiting patiently is easy. The answer you hear most of the time is that waiting is inherently frustrating and causes even the most faithful person to doubt.

As parents, we teach our children the importance of waiting, as they have a "right now" ideology which conflicts with reality. Despite their belaboring request for a new gadget or a new pair of tennis shoes, we often make them wait before we concede to their demands. However, as adults when we are forced to wait we portray childlike behavior and demand that God deliver us from our circumstances immediately. So even as adults, the frustration of waiting does not diminish. Consequently, we sometimes lose hope.

According to the Bible, David believed he would have succumbed to his trials had it not been for his hope in the Lord. In fact, he claims we should exhibit courage and strength during our waiting period. The Bible says "no one" who hopes in the Lord "will ever be" put to shame. The two words, "no one," and the phrase "will ever be" represent the depth of God's promise.

Today despite the gravity of your circumstance or the duration of your waiting period, you must be assured that God will not put your waiting in Him to shame. Just as David had courage, you too must have courage in the Lord. It is better to die in hope than to live in fear. Instead of allowing the wait to cause frustration, fear, and doubt, you must gain strength, courage, and hope. Your breakthrough is near. If you would just hold on, you would see your dreams materialize. Just ask Sarah the elderly mother, Moses the stuttering leader, or Jesus the wounded warrior, if there is hope is waiting.

CAN YOU SAY OVERFLOW?

> He got into one of the boats, the one belonging to Simon, and asked him to put out a little from shore. Then he sat down and taught the people from the boat. When he had finished speaking, he said to Simon, "Put out into deep water, and let down the nets for a catch." Simon answered, "Master, we've worked hard all night and haven't caught anything. But because you say so, I will let down the nets." When they had done so, they caught such a large number of fish that their nets began to break. So they signaled their partners in the other boat to come and help them, and they came and filled both boats so full that they began to sink.   Luke 5:3-7

One of the greatest tests Christians face is remaining in faith when they have seemingly exhausted all of their options. It is easy to boast about the goodness of God when your life is going well. But life can be just as turbulent as the ocean's waves. It is in those times that we must possess the greatest faith.

The family who has two children in college, but can no longer afford their monthly expenses due to an unexpected illness of one of the par-

LIFE LESSONS FROM MY FATHER

ents, must remain in faith. The middle-aged person laid off from their job after twenty years of service must remain in faith. The aspiring entrepreneur who invested five years in their business venture, only to watch it go under, must remain in faith. And yes, the fisherman who worked all night to no avail must remain in faith.

Today you must make a conscious decision to divorce yourself from fear, doubt, and worry, they only restrict your ability to have faith that God will deliver. The family with the two children mentioned above waited in faith, and God delivered, as someone heard their story and paid their monthly expenses until the parent recovered from their illness. The laid off worker was contacted by a company where they never applied and received a job offer that nearly doubled their salary. For the fisherman, it is written that he caught so many fish that his net began to break, and the boat began to sink.

We must unequivocally understand that we serve a God of abundance. He will pour out a blessing so massive that you will not have enough room to store it. Can you say "overflow?"

No Need to Look Back

Thus he overthrew those cities and the entire plain, destroying all those living in the cities—and also the vegetation in the land. But Lot's wife looked back, and she became a pillar of salt.

Genesis 19:25-26

In the desert the whole community grumbled against Moses and Aaron. The Israelites said to them, "If only we had died by the

Lord's hand in Egypt! There we sat around pots of meat and ate all the food we wanted, but you have brought us out into this desert to starve this entire assembly to death."   Exodus 16:2-3

We have a tendency to look back at the past, at the expense of not being grateful for our present reality. How many times have you been around someone who spends the majority of their time talking about past hurt and happiness? The conversation starts with, "Do you remember when …" or "I can't believe …" but always stays in a reflective moment, never giving attention to the present. Now there are some who will contend that reminiscing is good and no different than remembering a lost loved one; that it is simply recounting things that brought you joy. On the surface, this seems perfectly normal. But if they would further investigate, they would discover that most people's journey backward is due to a perceived reality of a present riddled with pain and an un-promising future. This ideology is flawed at best because we serve a God who is our present help. To turn our minds and efforts backward represents our lack of faith that God has a brighter future ahead.

Perhaps you are single, and an old acquaintance periodically calls. Instead of you thinking that situation is unfruitful, you revisit the past and attempt to rekindle the relationship, only to find yourself even more hurt and disappointed. However, we do not serve a God who plays life on rewind. He has the capability to fast-forward your circumstances into a miracle.

Now some will say, "But Jesus went backward to raise Lazarus." However, you must understand that He waited hours on purpose, allowing

Lazarus to die in order to raise him from the dead and show the power of the Father in the present moment. Lazarus did not awake talking about yesterday's miracles. He was focused on the present. Perhaps a married couple is having a myriad of problems and has seemingly exhausted their options. But instead of being totally committed to healing their broken marriage, they both begin to call old friends. Before you know it, they have allowed outside forces to further weaken their marriage. Your blessing cannot be found with a backward mentality.

The Israelites were being brought out of a tumultuous existence as slaves. But in their weakened state, they looked back on the food they had and desired to return to slavery, not focusing on the Promised Land, which was ahead. Even if Pharaoh had provided them with a king's feast, they still would have been slaves and would have had to endure his cruelty. In a real sense, freedom comes at a price, and many of the Israelites were unwilling to pay it, despite God continually showing them His protection.

Perhaps a youth who is uprooted from a dangerous environment misses their friends and desires to return to the old neighborhood because the students at their new school are not friendly. Just like Lot's wife, the youth is looking back. They are not realizing that God brought them out of destruction, and looking or going back will lead to their downfall. Today you must make a vow not to allow past brief moments of happiness to rob you of your destiny. God says to that husband and wife, "That old relationship did not work because I blocked it. The marriage, while rocky, is still covered by My hand." He says to that young child, "Despite you being in the midst of gunfire, I served as your shield of protection." To each one of us, He says, "If you truly knew that it was I, the Alpha and Omega, the beginning and the end, Your Lord and Your God, and Your present help in times of trouble, you would undoubtedly understand that there is no need to look back."

CONCEIT: A FALSE SENSE OF POWER

I must go on boasting. Although there is nothing to be gained, I will go on to visions and revelations from the Lord. I know a man in Christ who fourteen years ago was caught up to the third heaven. Whether it was in the body or out of the body I do not know—God knows. And I know that this man—whether in the body or apart from the body I do not know, but God knows—was caught up to paradise and heard inexpressible things, things that no one is permitted to tell. I will boast about a man like that, but I will not boast about myself, except about my weaknesses. Even if I should choose to boast, I would not be a fool, because I would be speaking the truth. But I refrain, so no one will think more of me than is warranted by what I do or say, or because of these surpassingly great revelations. Therefore, in order to keep me from becoming conceited, I was given a thorn in my flesh, a messenger of Satan, to torment me. Three times I pleaded with the Lord to take it away from me. But he said to me, "My grace is sufficient for you, for my power is made perfect in weakness." Therefore I will boast all the more gladly about my weaknesses, so that Christ's power may rest on me. That is why, for Christ's sake, I delight in weaknesses, in insults, in hardships, in persecutions, in difficulties. For when I am weak, then I am strong.   2 Corinthians 12: 1-10

We live in a world that places a high premium on success and its benefits, which for some creates a false sense of reality. When you are the CEO of a multi-billion dollar corporation and the majority of your life is spent on private planes headed to meetings and illustrious vacations, it can distort your sense of self. This reality is commonplace for many of the rich elite, royalty, and those who have achieved extreme financial success.

But how is it that you can have every material thing at your disposal but feel such loneliness and powerlessness? We have heard stories of celebrities, athletes, and politicians who have succumbed to the pitfalls of success, finding themselves in the most precarious of situations, ranging from adultery to murder despite their affluence. Power is relative. Those in some of the poorest of circumstances, be they economic or social, clamor at the chance of possessing power as they define it, even if their rich counterparts would see it as unworthy. Moreover, those who live in communities riddled by violence, gangs, and criminal activity still experience the same desires for power as those from backgrounds that are more affluent but how it manifests can differ greatly.

In a real sense, we all are like Paul, given a thorn which serves as a constant reminder of our external weaknesses in an effort to expose the internal power of God that lives on the inside of us. But oftentimes we fail to realize that His grace is sufficient. Like Paul, we must delight in our weaknesses, insults, hardships, persecutions, and the difficulties of life by relying on the strength and power of God.

Today be honest about your thorns. Do not complain, for they were strategically placed by God. The thorn of success, education, wisdom, unemployment, losing a loved one, failure, poverty, insecurity, and countless others serve as opportunities for us to humble ourselves and seek strength greater than our own. No matter how great your accomplishments, do not allow conceit to give you a false sense of power, for even the greatest among us will ultimately fall.

GET INTO POSITION

> Just then a woman who had been subject to bleeding for twelve years came up behind him and touched the edge of his cloak. She said to herself, "If I only touch his cloak, I will be healed." Jesus turned and saw her. "Take heart, daughter," he said, "your faith has healed you." And the woman was healed at that moment.
>
> Matthew 9:20-22

Jesus had performed many miracles, ranging from raising the dead to restoring sight to the blind. But this particular woman represented a great example of faith. Imagine having an illness for twelve years and despite all of your efforts, the pain never went away. She, like thousands of her time, had heard that a man named Jesus of Nazareth had performed many miracles. She like thousands of others wanted to see Him. Her determination and faith were greater than her illness and the thousands of people who gathered to see Jesus. Her tenacity to press forward was seen by Jesus as a great demonstration of faith. The moment she touched Him, He felt her affliction and instantly healed the woman. But her healing did not come until she got into position.

A common event at an American wedding reception is the tossing of the bouquet. Once the bride announces it, all the single women line up in anticipation of catching the ultimate prize. Like women at a wedding reception, the woman with the issue of blood understood that in order to receive God's blessings, you must get into position. Today despite your circumstance, you must have faith in God to provide deliverance. You cannot allow those around you to be a distraction. Instead, allow your trust in God to be the ultimate demonstration of your faith. Like a wide receiver in the National Football League, an outfielder in Major League Baseball, or even a woman giving birth, you must get into position for God to bless you. Are you ready? Are you determined? Are you willing to run through the crowd? If so, then get into position to receive your miracle.

FAITH TO THE FINISH

Now faith is confidence in what we hope for and assurance about what we do not see.   Hebrews 11:1

It is easy to have faith that you will receive a paycheck, given that you have worked and adhered to all the payroll requirements. It is equally easy to have faith that you will receive a high mark on a multiple-choice take-home exam, given that you have answered all the questions correctly. However, having faith that you will gain admittance to a top tier university or that you will receive a needed organ transplant takes a greater level of confidence.

Noah had to have faith that rain, which he had never seen, would come. Moses had to have faith that God would deliver the Promised Land, which he had never seen. The three wise men had to have faith to follow a bright star to meet a child that they had never seen. Jesus had to have faith that He would rise, which He had never seen. As you approach those things that you are hoping will materialize, be assured that life will present you with doubt, distractions, and disbelief. But God will provide if you remain in faith. Be aware that how God provides will not always be as you had hoped, but it will always be greater than you expected. You hoped for the transplant, but God gave you immeasurable peace and miraculously rejuvenated your organ without surgery or medicine. As for the admittance to the top tier university, you received a denial letter but two weeks later, you received an acceptance letter from an Ivy League school in which you were sure you had no chance of being accepted. When the organ donors did not match, you were not discouraged, and when the denial letter came, you were not dismayed. But you remained in faith, and God emphatically delivered.

Today the request is simple: you must remain in faith. The bank account is depleted, the house is in foreclosure, and no job leads are pending. Whatever the circumstance and no matter how dire the situation, those who are ultimately successful demonstrate faith to the finish.

WRESTLE WITH GOD

So Jacob was left alone, and a man wrestled with him till daybreak. When the man saw that he could not overpower him, he touched the socket of Jacob's hip so that his hip was wrenched as he wrestled with the man. Then the man said, "Let me go, for it is daybreak." But Jacob replied, "I will not let you go unless you bless me."   Genesis 32:24-26

You can spend a great deal of unproductive time with individuals who you believe are capable of fixing your current situation. How many hours have you been on the telephone with a friend, crying uncontrollably about your pressing issues, and despite their efforts of comfort and compassion your situation did not change? Perhaps you have been talking with one of your supervisors about a possible promotion, but despite their advice and counsel, you did not receive the position. As you lay next to your spouse compassionately pleading for them to help resolve the issues of your marriage, you have not found a feasible resolution.

Trying to change our situations by relying on man is not advantageous. The Bible reveals that prior to Jacob wrestling with God, he separated himself from his wives, servants, children, and possessions. Honestly, when you wrestle with God, you cannot allow yourself to be distracted by anything or anyone. Jacob possessed a grip of faith and refused to let God go until He blessed him. Jacob's demonstration of faith brings us parenthetically to another question, which is why are we so hesitant to wrestle with God? After Jacob's physical exertion and unwillingness to let go, God blessed him, for He knew that Jacob was prepared to wrestle without ceasing.

We are quick to say we want out of our afflictions, but we hardly make any sacrifices or demonstrations of faith that support our utterances. Wrestling is a sport of extreme skill. You must exude great strength and technique. A superior wrestler understands that they have to have a great stance and ultimately a great hold if they desire to overtake their opponent. Today you can seek the false comfort of friends, you can partner with people who you believe have power to remedy your affliction, or you can wrestle with the One who desires to bless you abundantly.

It is important you tell your spouse, children, family, friends, colleagues, and those whom you have wrestled with before that you will no longer take residence in their ability to resolve your issues, but have decided to take your struggles to the ultimate power source. If you desire true deliverance, it is time you wrestle with God.

So like an inquisitive yet humble student, we must be willing to always learn the life lessons from our Father as they will undoubtedly continue. Therefore, we must embrace each lesson as a gift no matter how difficult it may seem because in our reflection we soon realize what our Father knows, "The wise are mightier than the strong, and those with knowledge grow stronger and stronger" Proverbs 24:5 NLT.

The End

For God so loved the world that he gave his one and only Son, that whoever believes in him shall not perish but have eternal life.   *John 3:16*

LIFE TO LEGACY LLC

Let us bring your story to life! Life to Legacy offers the following publishing services: manuscript development, editing, transcription services, ghostwriting, cover design, copyright services, ISBN assignment, worldwide distribution, and eBooks.

Throughout the entire production process, you maintain control over your project. Even if you have no manuscript, we can ghostwrite your story for you from audio recordings or legible handwritten documents. Whether print-on-demand or trade publishing, we have publishing packages to meet your needs. We make the production and publishing processes easy for you.

We also specialize in family history books, so you can leave a written legacy for your children, grandchildren, and others. You put your story in our hands, and we'll bring it to literary life!

Please visit our website:
www.Life2Legacy.com

Or call us at:
877-267-7477

You can also e-mail us at:
Life2Legacybooks@att.net

www.ingramcontent.com/pod-product-compliance
Lightning Source LLC
Chambersburg PA
CBHW021337090426
42742CB00008B/640